On Acting

Mary Luckhurst is a playwright, translator and Lecturer in Modern Drama at the University of York. She co-edited *On Directing*, also by Faber, and wrote *The Drama Handbook* with John Lennard for Oxford University Press.

Chloe Veltman is a San Francisco-based correspondent for the *Daily Telegraph*. She is also a freelance theatre critic.

On Acting

INTERVIEWS WITH ACTORS

edited by Mary Luckhurst and Chloe Veltman

faber and faber

First published in 2001
by Faber and Faber Limited
3 Queen Square London WC1N 3AU
Published in the United States by Faber and Faber Inc.
an affiliate of Farrar, Straus and Giroux LLC, New York

Typeset by Faber and Faber Ltd
Printed in England by Clays Ltd, St Ives plc

ISBN 0-571-20656-5

10 9 8 7 6 5 4 3 2 1

For my father, Bernard Luckhurst, with thanks for all my childhood trips to the theatre

And for Anatoly Smeliansky, the most inspiring of teachers

Contents

Introduction

All of us can name actors whom we admire, but few of us know what goes into creating a performance; actors such as Laurence Olivier, Anthony Hopkins and Meryl Streep are icons, yet we rarely think about the art behind the star. We take performances on stage and screen at face value and pay little attention to questions of rehearsal process, technique and research. How does an actor prepare for a role? How does an actor relate to their director? Why go on stage at all? Is training necessary, or is there such a thing as genius? These are some of the questions that this book addresses.

There is still a certain mystique about craft, and actors are rarely asked to describe their process. Celebrity interviews in the media often concentrate on an actor's private life or focus on the commercial aspects of their latest project. Commentary on the way a play or film has been created is most usually sought from the director, who is considered to be the authority on artistic conception. The forerunner to this book, *On Directing*, examines theatre-making from the director's point of view; and inevitably, many directors talk about acting and actors. But it is the actor who has to perform and who is largely responsible for making the play or film a success. It seemed logical, therefore, to hear the actors' side of the story. This book focuses on actors whose roots lie in the theatre, though many also have a profile in film.

Today's greater awareness of different acting styles has been brought about by the exchange of ideas between cultures, the increase in international festivals and touring companies and the growth of acting schools. Before the Russian actor and director Konstantin Stanislavsky (1863–1938) developed a system of actor training, actors in the West simply learned the skills of their trade from their peers. Stanislavsky's ideas had enormous influence all over Europe and America. For the first time, someone had identified a range of specific skills needed by an actor both to understand a naturalist play and to perform it. In other words, he gave the craft of acting an explicit vocabulary. Stanislavsky's endeavour to describe the actor's craft influenced many practitioners: Lee Strasberg (1901–82) developed his own school of thought, the Method school of acting, as did Stella Adler, Sanford Meisner and

Richard Boleslavsky. There were, however, other practitioners who were influenced not so much by Stanislavsky's practice as by the desire to formalize their own approaches. This has been particularly true of post-1960s practitioners such as Jacques Lecoq, Jerzy Grotowski and Peter Brook, who have all explored non-text-based as well as text-based performance.

We wanted to reflect the diversity of approaches to acting, from the classical to the experimental, so this book contains twenty interviews with a wide range of actors of different generations. We interviewed actors who work predominantly in Britain and/or America because there is significant cross-fertilization between the two nations. While British actors have for a long time made appearances in American films and on Broadway, it is now fashionable for American actors to appear on West End stages. This trend has brought Kathleen Turner (*The Graduate*), Kevin Spacey (*The Iceman Cometh*) and Dustin Hoffman (*The Merchant of Venice*) to London, and taken Judi Dench (*Amy's View*), David Suchet (*Amadeus*) and Janet McTeer (*A Doll's House*) to New York.

Whilst we are cautious of making generalizations, we have noticed certain recurring preoccupations. The American actors we interviewed were more inclined to mention Stanislavsky and his disciples. Strasberg's Method is frequently cited and clearly marks an important historical referent for Americans. The Method grew out of Strasberg's understanding of Stanislavsky's system and focused on developing the actor's emotional impulses. While Stanislavsky's influence is felt in Britain, it has not had anything like the same impact; this may be because Strasberg's theory is more suited to the realistic requirements of film and television, which are traditionally more dominant media in the States. Broadly speaking, American actors seem more conscious of the influence of particular schools and methods than the British, who refer to individual teachers and practices, but not with the same fervour. British actors have traditionally begun their careers on stage, but because it is rarely possible to make a living from theatre acting alone, young British actors now tend to do film work at a much earlier stage in their careers. In America, where many actors have never been on stage, it is not uncommon for successful screen actors to turn to theatre as a way of adding to their credentials.

We tried to select a range of actors with different backgrounds; the oldest, Luba Kadison, was on stage during the First World War, while the youngest, Ayşan Çelik, began her professional career in the late

1990s. We also wanted to represent a variety of acting influences and philosophies; some actors have been heavily marked by their drama-school training, while others have developed their art on the job. Simon Callow considers his training at The Drama Centre in London to have played a vital part in his career, whereas Annabel Arden is fiercely opposed to conventional drama schools. The influence of Method-school acting is undeniable, but individual actors have strong opinions about other practical approaches. Elaine Stritch does not know if there is a technique of acting, but argues that there is a discipline. William H. Macy is a fervent proselytizer of David Mamet's system of 'Practical Esthetics' and Conrad Nelson believes in studying all kinds of practices and selecting the most useful elements from each.

The actors in this book think of their craft very differently. Michael Sheen argues that acting is not a profession but a vocation; Antony Sher delights in the transformations he can effect on stage; Linda Marlowe experiences an extraordinary buzz from performing live; Willem Dafoe sees the actor's job as 'doing' and 'being' the story; and Danny Hoch is motivated by a politics of social responsibility. A major theme throughout the interviews is the dichotomy between genius and craft. Some actors insist on the importance of instinct and impulse, whereas others believe that an actor can only develop through rigorous discipline.

It is perhaps surprising that few of the actors name other actors as role models. Just as Anna Deavere Smith has been more influenced by figures such as the opera singer Jessye Norman and the artist Pablo Picasso, so Barb Jungr has been inspired by musicians, singers and rock bands such as The Who. Eve Ensler was motivated to go on stage for the first time when she heard the powerful testimonies of the women she interviewed for *The Vagina Monologues*, whereas Ruth Posner's life was changed when she discovered Martha Graham's radical approach to dance.

Physical appearance is felt by many actors to have far too great a bearing on their career. Indira Varma expresses frustration at the type-casting she comes across in the film industry and Hugh Quarshie rages against the racial exclusivity of the theatre industry. Miriam Margolyes feels that actresses with unconventional looks are too often denied leading parts, while Liev Schreiber feels that looks and charm can too often advance an actor beyond their technical capability.

Appearance is not the only frustration. Many established actors have a desire to display the range of their skills and want real theatrical challenges; dissatisfied with the roles they are typically offered, they have taken the initiative and developed one-man or one-woman shows. Simon Callow and Miriam Margolyes have enjoyed tremendous success with their shows based on Charles Dickens's work, Linda Marlowe has received critical acclaim for her show *Berkoff's Women* and Elaine Stritch has created a one-woman show based on her own life. The one-person show is also a popular form for its own sake. Anna Deavere Smith and Danny Hoch choose to express themselves primarily through solo performance, whilst the success of Eve Ensler's *The Vagina Monologues* has inspired the author–performer to write another one-woman show.

There are as many definitions of acting as there are actors; it is variously described as 'dancing the hornpipe with fetters on', 'a basic form of human behaviour – something we all do', 'slaying the dragon', 'a form of portraiture', 'an ancient social event', 'telling stories', 'learning your lines and not bumping into the furniture' and, perhaps most bizarrely, 'a perfumed fart'. We hope you enjoy reading about these actors as much as we enjoyed speaking to them.

Mary Luckhurst and Chloe Veltman
London, 2000

Annabel Arden

Annabel Arden was born in London in 1959. In 1983 she formed the internationally acclaimed company Theatre de Complicite with Simon McBurney and Marcello Magni. As an actress, deviser and director she has been associated with many of its most celebrated productions: *The Visit* (1989), *The Three Lives of Lucie Chabrol* (1994), *The Street of Crocodiles* (1992–9), *The Winter's Tale* (1990) and *Out of a house walked a man* (1994). Complicite's work has won many awards, including Olivier Awards in many categories in Britain. Annabel Arden co-directed *The Women of Troy* (1991) and *India Song* (1993) with Annie Castledine at the Royal National Theatre. She also directs opera and her productions include: *The Magic Flute* (1994), *The Return of Ulysses* (1995), *Leonore* (1996), *Faust* (1996), *Der Zwerg* (1998) and *La Traviata* (1999).

What was your training?
I didn't have formal drama-school training. I began acting at school and at Cambridge University, where I met Simon McBurney. After university, I visited Simon in Paris, where he was training at the Ecole Jacques Lecoq; in Paris, I met Philippe Gaulier and Monika Pagneux, both of whom made a real impact on me, and whenever I had the chance to do a workshop with them, I took it. I am still a disciple of Monika's today, continue to be taught by her and have always found her teaching of movement revelatory. I bring her in to work with the actors and singers on all my productions, and she is also doing some retraining for members of Theatre de Complicite. Monika is now in her seventies, is German, and initially trained as a dancer in Berlin under the legendary Mary Wigman. She experienced the explosion of theatre in Europe after the war, worked in the circus and went to Paris to work with the French mime artists Etienne Decroux and Marcel Marceau. She was Jacques Lecoq's movement teacher for ten years and has worked with Peter Brook for many years. I have absorbed her influences, which are very mixed and decidedly continental.

What is it about Pagneux's movement teaching that you find revelatory?
She seeks to integrate the body and the imagination. For Monika, the

body is a like a musical instrument and she demands an extraordinary precision, at the same time linking movement to creative play and play-fulness. She worked with Moshe Feldenkreis's method of movement and found it revolutionized her thinking. The Feldenkreis method cer-tainly blew my mind when I first came across it; there's an extreme effi-ciency and economy about the movements and you can feel your body freeing up as you move, especially the back. There's often a horrible moment for actors when they realize that they have to leave the safety of preparation exercises and get on with acting and rehearsals. Performers who work with Monika are 'in play' from the beginning. I can only describe it as an interior play: much of it involves listening to yourself and others, and learning how listening transmutes into the imagination.

Monika is able to find a way of releasing full expression of the creative self through the body. She enables the body to become a rich source of different landscapes: your body sings, one moment you are a rock, or a heathland, or a nomad in the desert. The central idea is transformation. No actor needs the perfect body; they need their body to be fully avail-able to them, working at maximum potential with the minimum of effort in the same way that an opera singer is required to hit the right notes all the time while making their art seem effortless. Monika insists on physi-ologically accurate body work, but the pupil is never made to feel that they can't do the movements or that their body is awkward. She teaches me how to be myself, how to cope with the body I have, and makes me think about how I learn. Actors who have become 'middle-aged' and simply rely on their voices sometimes disillusion me. I want to know how to retain my fire. I think great actors like Alec Guinness and Ralph Richardson retained their mental and physical agility by instinct, but most of us need to work to keep ourselves fresh. Monika has asked me to be one of the people who carries on her teachings and I do feel that I should take up the baton, but at present I have many interests in other areas.

Your interest in continental theatre implies that you were discontented with the situation in England.
I've never liked the idea of formal drama school; I've never much liked institutions. It seemed to me that successful actors had to have certain classic looks – especially women – and I wasn't interested in that. When I met Simon in the 1970s, we were both making our own work and we both had a strong sense that English theatre lacked a non-literary bent.

Tadeus Kantor and Max Wall were both of equal interest to me; I thought the theatre and performance canons needed rewriting, and I didn't want to study mainstream practice. I've never lost the desire to tackle classical play texts, but I wanted to learn about other approaches to performance too. I was very inspired by David Gothard's reign at the Riverside Studios, where I saw a succession of physically very exciting continental groups like Els Comediants and La Claca, and it seemed natural to look outside England for inspiration.

I also learned on the job and formed part of a socialist feminist theatre collective called The 1982 Theatre Company, along with Neil Bartlett, Alan Scholfield, Annie Griffin and others. We lived on the dole and made political theatre, producing plays very much out of sheets and string. What fired me was the inventiveness of our productions, direct contact with the audience and politics. The outrage we felt at Margaret Thatcher's election in Britain in 1979 provided a good deal of impetus, and the miners' strike and the Falklands War also motivated us.

You have predominantly worked in ensembles as an actor. Why?
From the beginning, I was interested in making my own theatre. I have always directed and if you come to theatre from the point of view of a theatre-maker, then your mentality is different. For me, it wasn't enough to say 'I want to be an actor'; I wanted to take responsibility for what was being said – that was the ethos of my upbringing and I couldn't ignore it. In an ensemble, actors are part of the interpretative decision-making and they have to create things as a team. I saw Jacques Charon's ensemble production of *A Flea in Her Ear* at the Old Vic theatre when I was nine or ten and it changed my life; I left thinking, I want to be in that cast. I was fascinated by the fact that the actors were all wonderful, regardless of how long they were on stage. Charon was a brilliant actor and *farceur* from the Comédie-Française and directed actors to be very physical about their emotions and very upfront. I've never had ambitions to be a star actor, and think I would have worked much more if I had been driven by that desire. I'm much more interested in the act of creation, and the apotheosis of that was Theatre de Complicite's *The Street of Crocodiles* (1992). We lived the play for seven years and at its peak we reached new heights as an acting ensemble; audiences thrilled to the exquisite communication we had with each other and the way that we lived in each others' hands.

(3)

Conversely, I played Sonya in Chekhov's *Uncle Vanya* (1993) in a non-ensemble production and I had no idea how to exist with actors of that kind. I was used to a completely different way of working and I couldn't understand the way they communicated with one another. I respected the actors, but from my point of view they all seemed to act with invisible lines drawn round them and most were unwilling to respond in different ways each night. I functioned badly, but to my mind it is not possible to play ninety-eight performances of Chekhov without re-rehearsal.

Can you describe the journey of ensemble work with Theatre de Complicite?
As an actor, you go into the project but you don't necessarily know what your role is – that's the first difficulty. The actor plays many things in rehearsal and research is undertaken in action. There is material, but no text. One might say: 'Let's play a scene where I do this and you do that' and you both try it out. There isn't initially much discussion amongst Complicite actors; we just keep trying things out. In the early work, we devised material and improvised dialogue round a theme. In *Anything for a Quiet Life* (1987) we wanted to do a show about fear, so we explored states of fear, ranging from mild anxiety to terror. We experimented with places which are often associated with fear, like hospital waiting-rooms, or scenes in the dark. We kept returning to scenes in offices as a place of fertile ideas and gradually characters began to coalesce.

For the later shows, we developed a pattern to the day: in the mornings, we worked physically and vocally as a group and we created large-scale, ensemble images like the wind, or the night, and dealt with questions of timing and making the images function. In the afternoons, we tended to do work which related more specifically to the play or text; for example, during *The Winter's Tale* (1990) rehearsals, we asked ourselves how we would do the sheep-shearing scene and we took props and set about inventing it. We do such exercises for weeks and end up with a plethora of material which it is up to the director to cut and shape. We never have a moment where we stand with the play in our hands; the understanding is that such work is done alone at home. Actors think through the arc of the character for themselves. Ensemble creation has no formal template and actors work in the dark for a long time. In *The Street of Crocodiles* we all had journeys to make as the characters, but there were dark spots in each journey; we found our own solutions and were often aware that although we as actors needed clarification of a point on our path, it was not important for the audience to know.

Ellen Terry described the art of acting as similar to 'dancing the hornpipe with fetters on'; somehow the actor has to be as nimble as possible even though their feet are in irons. Ensemble acting demands very quick thinking and the ability to have your mind focused on several different levels at once; an actor may be lifting a heavy desk, flicking a switch, trying to catch a spoon and playing the scene all at the same time. Discipline is the only answer; if an opera singer has to sing B flat, then no other note will do, and the actor's art must be as musically precise and free as the singer's. Marcello Magni is famous in Complicite for his extraordinary dexterity with objects: he really is a magician and can often find a way of making an object disappear from the stage. Actors are often nervous of props, but in Complicite we want to overcome all those very English fears of space, objects and physicality.

Complicite is a company that is designed to support creative chaos and that is a luxury. It's a profligate way of generating material and we always have far too much. By contrast, I think that actors in traditional theatre shows often feel the time-pressure and are forced to take short cuts and make compromises and over-hasty decisions in their performance, and as a result they box themselves in and fail to stretch themselves. We have many controls and tests in Complicite and we often talk of 'testing' material, whether it's watching each other or testing out a gag – Simon has a background in stand-up comedy and has an acute sense of timing.

What qualities does the ensemble actor need?
You need incredible stamina as an ensemble actor; you work with the same group of people all the time and the rehearsal room resounds with many voices and many concerns. You have to be generous and able to abandon ego. You also need a strong visual sense, which you acquire by doing, making, and acting as each other's mirror. Over time, you develop an interior eye and you begin to know what your movement looks like from a spectator's perspective. You also develop a physical memory and have a sense not just of where you are in the space but what your spatial relationship is to everyone else. You must be able to do, to make. Max Wall is a hero of mine because he played Beckett brilliantly, but he didn't start acting in a conventional way: he began by singing for

his supper and inventing pratfalls. Yoshi Oida, who has worked with Peter Brook, has a magical, spiritual stage presence but is fascinated by precision and physical trickery.

Acting is simultaneously about freedom and precision. It is not about self-expression as such: as a director, I'm not interested in an actor's personality, I'm interested in what that actor can do. 'Feedback' is currently a fashionable idea at many drama schools and in too many cases it turns into a forum for actors to talk about their feelings; in my view, actors must have achieved something in their performance to earn that right. An actor's feelings are important to an extent, but too many students are encouraged to think that their personal emotions are part of the work and that is not what performance is about: there is a certain distance one must maintain at the same time as being passionately involved – one must be present but detached. A professional actor knows when they have performed badly in a show, knows when they have let others down – going home with that burden is part of an actor's life. I probably sound hard, but I do think that a certain liberal 'mushiness' is affecting standards; teachers must insist that their students set high goals for themselves.

You've been directing opera recently. What has drawn you to it?
I think contemporary opera tends to be more radical than much contemporary theatre. Complicite's work has always had music running through it and theatre is in essence about time and rhythm. *The Street of Crocodiles* was operatic in the sense that the pitch of emotion was very high and our movements were melodramatic. Melodrama is undervalued and misunderstood, and sometimes it is the only level of expression which is appropriate to the text. I have a love–hate relationship with opera but am fascinated by the voice and think it is a most mysterious attribute. The performance standards demanded of an opera singer are extremely high and I enjoy the exactness as well as the multi-dimensionality of it as an art. An opera singer can totally transport an audience with their voice, and the power of that skill transfixes me. The most amazing performances in opera occur when you forget that the singer is singing. Literally, the thoughts and emotions, the gesture and the action are so absolutely the interpretation of the music that you think the person is speaking. I recently saw Anja Silja play the Kostelnicka in *Jenufa* at Glyndebourne and I practically couldn't breathe whenever she was on. I have had exactly the same experience with great acting. Opera is

difficult to act because you have to sing and you do not control the tempo – the conductor does. Acting is difficult because you have to create the music which is the text: there is no orchestra behind you. If you slow down, there is no one breathing fire from the pit.

You directed one of the most innovative plays of the twentieth century, Marguerite Duras's India Song, *which makes very unusual demands on the actors. Could you talk about that?*

I co-directed the show with Annie Castledine. The play was originally commissioned by the National Theatre, but the experimental nature of it made it a risk and we did the première at Theatre Clywd, Wales. It's a play in which not a word is spoken by any of the performers; Duras's stage directions explicitly state that 'not a word is spoken on the stage'. We chose to realize her extensive text in voice-over, with a precisely choreographed physical text on stage. We had limited means and could not record the sound tape until we were well into rehearsals, so we worked with the actors imagining the voices, reading the text out to them first and then working in silence. We concentrated hard on getting actors to listen and respond to words through movement: does the sound precipitate a large or small movement? Is it rapid or slow? In terms of movement, we worked with the aesthetic of unbearable heat because the play is set in Indochina; we communicated our vision to the actors with pictures and photographs of India and East Asia. Heat slows down responses and we worked on creating a very sensuous, hypnotic effect; actors were in the position of learning to speak eloquently with their bodies, not their mouths. The production was extraordinary and trance-like, and audience members talked of sensory overload and how they had simply abandoned themselves to an overwhelming visual and aural experience. It was not an event which was logically absorbable in the conventional sense of theatre and this troubled critics a great deal; I was frustrated by the critical bafflement, because we abandon ourselves to music without demanding logical explanations but it seems that our assumptions about theatre as an experience are quite ingrained. Simon McBurney hit a similar problem with Complicite's *The Winter's Tale*: he did not play Leontes in a traditional way and some critics felt that certain 'Shakespearean standards' had been infringed. Leontes is not a 'logical' character; he is consumed by a sudden attack of grotesque, inexplicable jealousy which has fearful consequences. The extraordinariness of the man must be realized and the extent of his mania must be revealed.

(7)

What is acting for you?

Acting is a basic form of human behaviour – we all do it. In its purest form, it is play. When a young child picks up a crumb from a table they are totally present in that moment and all their energy and focus is directed towards picking up the crumb. Actors need to bring that degree of presence and concentration to their performances. There was a time when the line from *King Lear* 'Never, never, never, never, never' was immediately identifiable by everyone, but theatre no longer has that cultural homogeneity. There was a time when theatre was about telling familiar stories, but the stories are now new and different and from many cultures. An actor is a master storyteller, who should be able to produce an effect of suspended time, and the best performances provide a charge of incredible force. Acting and theatre are a means of coming together and examining what it means to be human; hitting the right physical notes and giving a great performance can change the lives of a few people in the audience, and that should be the aim of all actors. It should also be, in the words of Ken Campbell – another great influence – 'a bit of a caper'.

Simon Callow

Simon Callow is an actor, director and writer. He was born in 1949, went to Queen's University, Belfast and trained at The Drama Centre, London. His many appearances as an actor include, in the theatre, *Arturo Ui* (Half Moon, 1978), *Amadeus* (National Theatre, 1979), *Faust* (Lyric Hammersmith, 1988), *The Alchemist* (Royal National Theatre, 1996), *The Mystery of Charles Dickens* (2000); on television, *La Ronde* (BBC), *David Copperfield* (BBC), *The Woman in White* (BBC); and the films *A Room with a View*, *Four Weddings and a Funeral* and *Amadeus*. He has directed plays, operas and musicals, including *Così Fan Tutte*, *Shirley Valentine*, *Carmen Jones* and *My Fair Lady*. His books include *A Difficult Actor: Charles Laughton*, *Shooting the Actor*, *Acting in Restoration Comedy* and *Being an Actor*.

You talk about the importance of training in your book Being an Actor. *What are your views now?*
My opinion remains the same: actors need a three-year training period to discover their strengths and weaknesses away from the public eye; they must be allowed to try out as much as possible and be permitted to make fools of themselves. There are two vital elements to the training: a contained environment and an integrated programme. The objective of the three years must be to increase an actor's expressiveness (though in my experience, most drama schools don't pursue this as a priority) in order to discover ways of offering images of the human condition which are as rich and challenging as possible.

You have expressed great concern about the need to allow actors room for their own creativity. Why?
I've always argued that it is possible for actors to be primary creative artists who try to realize the author's intentions, but directors far too rarely provide opportunities for actors to function as creative artists. A few actors have the gift of being able to push their expressiveness to a very wide extent: Charles Laughton was certainly capable of it, and Mark Rylance, the Artistic Director of the Globe Theatre, reaches for an almost poetic intensity of performance. Three roles immediately

come to mind for which I was given the space to take huge leaps of imagination to make the characters come alive: Arturo Ui in Brecht's *The Resistible Rise of Arturo Ui*, Molina in Puig's *Kiss of the Spider Woman* and Mozart in Peter Shaffer's *Amadeus*.

How do you set about working on your roles?
I always try to find the archetypal in a character. For example, in the film *A Room With a View* I played the Reverend Beebe, who seemed to exude benevolence in the script. I asked myself what it might mean to be a priest. I have a Catholic background and earlier in my life wanted to become a priest myself, so I'm moved, as many people are, by the thought of a goodly priest. Much of my work is unmethodical; I tried to dwell in Beebe's character, to submit to his ideas and his impression of the world. I asked myself what the sensation was of my own benevolence and endeavoured to amplify it. I drive these inquiries to quite an extreme, so that I'm not just getting a glimpse of a character but a bucketful! My overwhelming image of Beebe was of a man who emitted a gentle, permeating light. I regularly find that music gives me a language for a character's physicality; I connected Elgar's *Dream of Gerontius* and its vision of paradise with Beebe because it is quintessentially English and because it has a radiant and heavenly quality.

I remember the power of a particular image when I was developing the role of Arturo Ui. I felt that Brecht had constructed him as semi-human and I aimed to be as frightening as possible. The idea I had of Ui was inspired by a description of cancer cells that I'd read, about when the cells break down and there is a destructive, floating energy.

There are times when I have real difficulties with a role. The first physical aspect I need to explore is voice, so I'm always in trouble if I can't get a sense of how a character speaks, if I can't imagine what sort of noises they would make, or hear the sound of their words in my head. When I played Molina, I simply couldn't get a sense of his voice and at the point of the first read-through had no idea how I would play it; in fact, I apologized to Mark Rylance, who was acting the other part, and said I would simply do a straight reading. Out of nowhere, I had a flash of inspiration and suddenly knew that I would play him like a moon-struck shop-girl, that he must have both a down-to-earth quality and a sense of mystery. In fact, that interpretation was the one I played right the way through the performance, but it did not come out of my self-questioning or my attempts at preparation. When Olivier played

Othello, he trained himself for six months to add an octave to his voice. I don't have that gift but it can be very frustrating to hear a character's voice in your head and then not be able to reach it in practice. I had trouble with Falstaff; in my imagination, his voice announced itself to me as several tones lower than was comfortable for my actual vocal range. I destroyed my voice in that production.

You're playing many characters in your current show, The Mystery of Charles Dickens. *How do you manage technically?*
In the same way that a musician has to strike the right note, actors should be able to throw a switch and hit the centre of a character at a split second's notice. I've achieved this facility through a great deal of personal training. Drama school opened me up and extended me vocally and imaginatively, but I've worked hard to develop ways of enabling my body to play sensation and impulse. I find that the important thing is not to feel a lot, but to feel it on demand. I always try to find the music of a character; for example, Dickens himself is a mix of Berlioz and Beethoven – Berlioz because of the jagged, irregular rhythm which proceeds in leaps and bounds, and Beethoven because of the steadfast, solid underpinning in his music.

At The Drama Centre, we were given ways of thinking about character in terms of time (intuition), space (intellect), flow (emotion) and weight (physicality). I work out which element predominates and what the balance of the elements might be: Dickens himself is weight plus flow, meaning solid and of the earth plus emotional. Mozart in *Amadeus* is a balance of time and flow, an intuitive and emotional man but not especially intellectual or grounded. What is critical when I play a character is the language they speak; I need to be given a strong sense of their linguistic world and a poorly written script affects my focus.

Do you train physically as well?
I keep fit and have a personal trainer. I've done Pilates in the past, which is a body-conditioning method that works deeply and specifically on the muscles. I make sure that my body is as available to me as possible. I've never cared overly about my appearance, but actors need to use their physicality in their art: James Robertson Justice's bulk was very much a part of his characterizations and Charles Laughton loathed his physical attributes but certainly knew how to use them.

How do you think acting has changed?

The crisis about acting at the moment revolves around the question of personality; in the past, acting had to be on a large scale: there was no microphone and no film close-up and actors constructed a persona which was larger than life, whether they were playing the patriarch, the villain or the lover. Some actors invented personas with many facets, and others with just a few: Ralph Richardson had one large extraordinary facet and Edith Evans developed a whole array of qualities. The system was different then. Actors were given parts that would develop their range and were ushered into their own kingdom. Edith Evans asked Michael Redgrave early on in his career who he was going to be like; what she meant was that while he might be influenced by certain actors, he should also develop something definite and distinct about his own style. Michael Gambon is an example of an actor who is like a mighty organ with many stops and who can bring both greatness and idiosyncrasy to a role. There aren't many actors like this any more. Many say that, in general, acting standards are much higher than they used to be, and no doubt there was a lot of old rope, but I miss the dinosaurs like Edith Evans and Sybil Thorndyke; they were still vigorous in the 1960s, though their styles were out of step with the times. Whilst John Gielgud simply 'played' a part, Olivier was a more modern actor in the sense that he built up a detailed psychological account of a character and asked what made them tick. He came from a long tradition of English and French actors who created a mask for a character. George Bernard Shaw famously divided actors into two sorts: the Classical actor, who becomes the character, and the Romantic actor, who makes the character become him.

You have written about the importance of observation for an actor. Why?

Observation and the study of human behaviour are vital for actors. I don't work so much by imitation, though there is much to be said for that kind of precision – I recently saw Russian actors from the Maly Theatre perform *The Possessed* and was very struck by the brilliance of their mimicry of particular moments. One actor sat down drunkenly and got the height of the chair wrong; it was a tiny detail, but beautifully observed. I think that one of the effects of Strasberg's teachings has been that actors are more and more keyed in to the internal dynamics of character and less and less attuned to external details like the example I've just given. Brecht's definition of an actor was someone who knows how to drink a cup of tea in twenty-seven different ways; in other words, he thought that even the pouring of a cup of tea could reveal something distinctive about the character. There's much truth in this: Gwendolen from Wilde's *The Importance of Being Earnest*, Lady Macbeth and Ophelia would all drink tea in entirely different ways!

What effect do you hope to have on an audience?
I want to illuminate character and human life and I by no means think that realism is the only way to do it.

Are you aware of any particular influences on your acting?
Early on in my career, I was interested in the projection of the self as grotesque and admired Olivier's representation of Richard III and Charles Laughton's portrayal of Quasimodo. My interest in the grotesque was, I suspect, a way of challenging the audience's love – despite the character I was playing, I wanted them to love my acting. Certain actors have interested me historically, but it is performances that linger in my mind. I saw Mark Rylance play Hamlet not too long ago and though his performance was erratic, it was also unforgettable. He constantly illuminated the play as if he were holding it up to the light. Hamlet can too often be played on a single note, but Mark's performance was wild, ferocious and funny. I don't know how he works, but the effect on me is that I will go back and wonder on it.

What do you tell your actors when you are directing?
Directing is akin to teaching, and I help elucidate things for actors. My directing is pragmatic and I do not have a system as such; I simply try to dig deeper and deeper. One of the directors I most admire is John Barton, who sounds out every single note in a text. I always say to actors that they should ask *what* a character is before they ask *who* he or she is. What is Hamlet? He is a prince, a scholar, a son and a bereaved man. Above all, this is what has to be played – adjectives should be used with caution and time cannot be wasted on what is not playable. I also want actors to think about their speeches, about phrasing and melody, so I ask why a particular speech or character should not be cut. They then have to defend the importance of their part or their words. I might ask actors to write the story of a play from their character's viewpoint in the first person, so that they have to think about their path through the play and their relationship to other characters. Other important questions

with which I confront actors are: what do you want to show, and why?
What would you like the audience to think and how do we achieve that?

Where would you like to head with your acting?
I would like to have the chance to play a character with depth and
expanse in a play: acting in Goethe's *Faust* was very challenging in that
sense. I also love playing the part of Henry Higgins in Shaw's *Pyg-
malion*, which I know I can play better than anyone else in the world.
I've always been drawn to ensemble playing, but the right conditions for
it do not exist in mainstream theatre in England. I could found a company but I can't imagine that I would ever find the funding for such an
enterprise. Working with like-minded actors committed to realizing a
play in the most potent way possible is the ultimate experience for me.

Ayşan Çelik

Born in 1975 in California, Ayşan Çelik, was educated at the University of California at Los Angeles (UCLA) School of Theater, Film and Television and the Harvard Institute for Advanced Theater Training, from which she graduated with a Masters degree in 1999. Working in conventional plays as well as devised and physical theatre, her New York credits include Musa in the New York première of Robert McGrath's *Hypatia* at the Soho Repertory Theater (2000), Lady Macbeth in *Macbeth* at the Mint Theater (2000), Frida Kahlo in Theater Mitu's *Project Frida* in New York (2001) and La Trista in Theater Mitu's *Catholica Book Two* (2000), both at the Lincoln Center's HERE Performance Café, and Clara in Theater Mitu's *But Above All, Without a Plan* (2000). Her work with the American Repertory Theater in Cambridge, Massachusetts, includes Antigone in Sophocles' *Antigone* (2000), Musa in the world première of *Hypatia* (1999), Kaja in Ibsen's *The Masterbuilder* (1999), Jessica in Shakespeare's *The Merchant of Venice* (1999) and the Teenage Greek Chorus in Paula Vogel's *How I Learned to Drive* (1998). She has also performed in the New Repertory Theater's production of Geoffrey Hatcher's adaptation of Henry James's *The Turn of the Screw* (2000) and as La Trista in *Catholica Book One* with Theater Mitu at the Mark Taper Forum Wing (1998). In 2002, she is playing the role of Jandhari in *The Mahabharata*, adapted by Ruben Polendo, at the McCarter Theater in Princeton, New Jersey.

What was your training as an actor and do you specialize in any particular acting technique?
I had a very mixed training. From the age of six, I did ballet and played the violin and piano. I went on to study acting at UCLA and at Harvard. When I was an undergraduate at UCLA, we began with a year of Method acting with Salome Jens, an exciting teacher. I do not substantially use the Method but find it helpful for defining 'want' and 'action'. Method stopped me from being embarrassed on stage or in rehearsal. Some of the exercises were focused on an actor's ability to share their private selves with an audience by drawing upon events taken from their life. Although I do not do this in practice, going through the training in class

was very valuable because if you want to be creative as an actor, you have to be prepared to make a fool of yourself; a year of sharing 'personal moments' with others helped me, if anything, get over fear. I think this is especially helpful to me now; when emotions come out, I am not embarrassed about them. I do not like focusing on emotion; it usually comes out after the physical and vocal work.

From the start, I have been interested in exploring physical extremes. I trained extensively with Jacques Heim, the founder of Diabolo Dance Theatre, in Los Angeles. My studies with him exposed me, for the first time, to using my body in other ways than highly controlled and choreographed dance. The benefits of this were exploring how to use my body, trusting myself and others physically, and taking both physical and psychological risks. For example, I would do exercises like leaping off a ten-foot wall into the arms of my classmates, or contact improvisation where we would work with each other's body weight, sometimes carrying and lifting. I think my work with Heim formed the basis of the very physical work that I am interested in now. Even if I am working on a play with no extra movement or choreography, learning to take physical risks with Heim has taught me to be braver about such things as using my instincts. I also acquired bravery through the street theatre and improvisation we did with Heim, sometimes working in public with an audience who did not know they were supposed to be an audience. Heim encouraged us to do things to intrigue the strangers around us, in cafés, on buses or in the street. Certainly we were directed to do this in a subtle way, so that we would not be a public annoyance, but once we got kicked off the Campus Express bus for creating a disturbance and I heard that Heim himself was arrested for dancing on the roof of a taxi in Paris.

I have had a mixture of movement training and I continue to take classes in forms that I am unfamiliar with. I did ballet for twelve years, as well as other dance forms for shorter periods, including flamenco, hip-hop and modern dance. I also studied biomechanics and Alexander Technique. Ruben Polendo and Margaret Eginton both had a great deal of influence over my physical development as an actor. Margaret taught me how to release my body and use every muscle. She taught me a lot about working from physical instincts and playing physical actions. Ruben, as a director, has always developed exercises in rehearsal that push me physically, making me realize the psychology of a moment in a play or a piece of dramatic action through physical action.

In graduate school at Harvard, I trained in Practical Esthetics with Scott Zigler and took classes with the Russian director Yuri Yeremin. Yeremin's training was useful for making us look deeper into a character and story, beyond our first impressions. We did a lot of Chekhov and I learned a great deal more about performing relatively naturalistic texts from him. The Russian training was also good for developing focus and discipline through a number of repetitive exercises focusing on such things as memory, timing and ensemble.

I got a lot out of training in Practical Esthetics with Scott. Personally, I think I am still figuring out exactly how I work, but I have come away from his class having learned to take the attention away from myself and focus on my partner. He taught me to trust my perceptions of what is happening in any given moment on stage and to find a way of acting extremes of behaviour in a believable way. Furthermore, this technique gave me the licence to let go of all preparation. Once I step on stage into a scene, I can let go and simply be present with my partner and I can trust that everything else, such as text analysis and choices about desire and action, is at work in my body and subconscious. Thus, I can act from my instincts and not my intellect. Scott was a perceptive teacher and although I do not practise this technique exclusively, I use what I found useful in it alongside other techniques.

I have a great admiration for and derive inspiration from those artists who work physically in theatre or dance, whether it be an ensemble of Bhuto artists or ballet dancers. I like using improvisation and coming up with completely new physical concepts and I am interested in developing a form that looks at every element from a physical perspective. In rehearsal, this means finding solely physical reactions to a story. What appear to be abstract physical movements are then transformed by the actor's deep engagement with the subject matter, and as long as the actor is engaged, then the audience will also be engaged and inspired by what they see. Even if the play I am working on does not call for extreme movement, I find that if I work through my body first and focus on what the character is doing physically and vocally, other things fall more easily into place. Certainly I have to do the intellectual work, but once I have done this work, staying in my body ultimately helps me make the most interesting choices, which are instinctual rather than intellectual ones.

How do you develop relationships with audiences?
The audience is the final element; the performers are the bridge between the story and the audience. Whether we are doing something completely recognizable to them or something of a very abstract nature, as long as we, the actors, are engaged, I think the audience will be too. Whatever we do, we must not alienate them.

What motivates you to act?
My need to act stems from the feeling that myths, legends and stories are not as important to people today as they once were. The tradition of storytelling goes back thousands of years and I want to continue that tradition. I was deeply affected by seeing a stage performance at the age of four. I was watching the actors up on stage and suddenly started to feel very strange; I could feel myself entering their story and I was completely engaged. That feeling has happened many times since, but it has never felt as strong as it did that one time. I do not necessarily think people should lose themselves when they see a live performance, but there is something to be said for being taken on a journey with an actor. Thinking back to that incident when I was four years old makes me, as an actor, want to create that experience for others.

What are the qualities in actors you most admire?
I know I am watching a great performance when I stop analysing what an actor is doing on stage and get taken in by the story they are telling. I actually forget that I am watching an actor. When I am watching a really powerful performance, I find it impossible to pin down what the actor is doing and the only thing I can describe about their performance is something superficial, like what dialect they are using.

Once an actress angered me by telling me that I had it easy. She meant it as a compliment, but I was indignant when she said that she had to work *so* hard whereas it was clearly effortless for me. How could she know how hard I worked? I do not believe that anything comes easily and I am somewhat sceptical about the idea of talent. I do not understand what it is. I can believe that it exists, but do not understand why. Suzuki, the Japanese music teacher and founder of the Suzuki Method, said 'talent is hard work'. There are probably actors out there who work their asses off and do not manage to succeed with a part or get offered roles. I do not completely understand why this happens; it may be as a result of the imbalanced ratio of actors to jobs. Ultimately, it does not help me to worry about talent; I don't know what it is and I have no control over however much I might or might not have. My brother, a software engineer, once told me when I was little that working hard is more important than being smart. Talent seems to be like intelligence in a way and the question of its existence can come down to the nature–nurture debate. At the end of the day, all I can do is work hard.

In terms of specific actors I admire, I very much like Daniel Auteuil, Isabelle Adjani, Simon Callow, Maggie Smith, Emma Thompson, John Turturro, Robert De Niro, Sidney Poitier, Catherine Deneuve, Judi Dench, Meryl Streep, Jay Rai, Gene Kelly, Donald O'Connor and Charlie Chaplin. In addition to actors, I am also impressed by other performers such as Björk, Pina Bausch, Laurie Anderson, Diamanda Galas, Philip Glass and Itzhak Perlman.

How much research do you undertake for a role?
It depends, but usually I try to do all my research before I begin rehearsing a play. I start by doing lots of reading and I gather images. I like to bombard myself with as many people's opinions, stories and pictures as I can, from which to inspire my own reactions. Recently my theatre company, Theatre Mitu, did a piece for the Chekhov Now Festival in New York. Collectively, we decided to construct a production inspired by Chekhov's short stories and vaudevillian short plays. The research we undertook for this project was tremendous: we read all his letters, stories and plays and found out everything we could about him and the environment in which he lived. We did research into vaudeville theatre, including the living circumstances of real vaudeville actors and the performance pieces they would execute, all with the goal of finding the connections between Chekhov's world and that of vaudeville theatre. We found pictures of vaudeville actors and each of us embodied a particular vaudevillian in our characters on stage. We also did improvisations based on and inspired by vaudeville scenes. This was the basis for creating our own piece on the subject.

Which directors inspire you to do your best work?
I need to be able to trust a director's eye, ear and heart. As an actor, I cannot watch myself on stage or in rehearsal. If I am struggling to do that, then I am being drawn away from my ability as an actor.

Ruben Polendo, the Artistic Director of Theatre Mitu, is a director I admire immensely. The rehearsal space he creates is sacred: it is a place for focus, creativity and risk. Without being dictatorial, he inspires love and respect between the actors whilst demanding focus and presenting a challenge. He is like one of those rare teachers who can push you to do your best work by creating a fearless environment. By ensuring that all the actors respect one another, we are never embarrassed about the creative process. He has developed a lot of creative exercises as the basis of projects, from physical improvisations to writing exercises. I feel I am being stretched the most when I work with him. He and I also have the advantage of having worked together for five years, which for me is a relatively long chunk of time to refine a creative relationship.

Scott Zigler is extraordinarily perceptive about the individual actor's habits and process. He is able to figure out what note to give an actor to extract a more believable performance. He sees the subtle changes needed to make an actor or scene compelling and I trust what he sees completely.

Other directors I admire include François Rochaix, Marcus Stern, Andrei Serban, Kate Whoriskey, Don Freuchte and Robert Brustein.

What would make you turn down a role?
At this stage in my career, I would probably only turn down a role if I had worked with that director in the past and had a bad experience; if I had not trusted their ability to direct or not trusted them personally. Having said that, if a role enabled me to be seen by more people or was a significant step in my career, I would probably do it, despite the director. I do not have a solid answer to this question; it would probably depend on the particular situation.

Who do you look to for criticism of your acting?
I have not been in the business long enough to have a relationship with what newspaper critics say about me and I do not read them much anyway; good or bad, they just freak me out. I would always trust what particular mentors have to say, teachers or directors whose opinions I respect. During graduate school, I also came to trust my flatmate, Shani, who was in law school at the time. Despite not having any formal training in theatre, she is always very perceptive about seeing the difference between what an actor is trying to do on stage and what they actually achieve; for example, when we go to see a play together, she will say something like, 'That actor was trying to look scary, but I didn't feel frightened.' She does not come from a theatre background, so she is not

coloured by a particular aesthetic, and she is very perceptive about behaviour on and off stage. I wish we still lived in the same city.

What are your plans for the future?
I am mainly interested in live performance. There are particular elements that can only be experienced between a live audience and actors on a stage. There are things to be discovered in live theatre but in order to survive it has got to evolve as an art form; to paraphrase Chekhov, 'We must have new forms; if not, we might as well have nothing.' If we try to preserve old forms alone, theatre will no longer be engaging. I want to be a part of the evolution of live theatre. I want to continue learning the craft of performing; I don't think that will ever finish. Beethoven said, in a letter to a young actress, that the artist is never satisfied.

Do you feel optimistic or pessimistic about the theatre industry as it stands?
There are a lot of things about the industry that concern me, but I have to focus on the parts that I might change for myself. There is no room for a fatalistic attitude in theatre; theatre has become less important to people's lives and many believe it is dying, but I have to grasp the factors contributing to its decline and see how I can turn them around, even if that means changing them only in a rehearsal room with a few other actors who have the same intent. Although we have other ways of telling stories, we will feel a terrible loss if live performance in the USA continues to lose its audience in places other than New York. I am determined to work with other artists towards finding a way of rekindling society's interest in live theatre.

When I was an undergraduate in Los Angeles, I watched Pina Bausch rehearse. It was the very first time I had come across work of an extremely physical, abstract nature. Regardless of the style, what I saw affected me about as deeply as that first experience I had at the age of four. I would like to make people feel like that about theatre and I know that somehow it is possible. Perhaps I am being overly optimistic, but believe me, I am not exactly free from dissatisfaction. Optimism and dissatisfaction can work hand in hand.

Willem Dafoe

Born in 1955 in Wisconsin, Willem Dafoe is a core member of the New York-based experimental theatre company The Wooster Group, alongside Kate Valk, Spalding Gray, Jim Clayburgh, Peyton Smith and the late Ron Vawter. Under the direction of Elizabeth LeCompte, The Wooster Group creates theatre and media pieces using sound, film, movement, classic texts and video and has won many awards, including National Endowment for the Arts, New York State Council for the Arts and the City Department of Cultural Affairs grants. In 1991, the Group was awarded an OBIE (Off Broadway Theatre Award), recognizing fifteen years of service to the arts. Dafoe's work with the group includes Eugene O'Neill's *The Hairy Ape* (1995) and *Emperor Jones* (1993); and *Brace Up!* (1991), based on Chekhov's *The Three Sisters*; *North Atlantic* by James Strahs (1984/99); and Racine's *Phèdre* (2000). On screen, Dafoe is probably best known for his Academy Award-nominated performance as Sgt Elias in *Platoon* (1986) and for his portrayal of Jesus in *The Last Temptation of Christ* (1988). Other notable screen roles include *Wild at Heart* (1990), *EXistenZ* (1999), *The English Patient* (1996), *Shadow of the Vampire* (2000) and *American Psycho* (2000).

How do you see your process of training as an actor?
I did not have any formal training. From a very early age, I have followed a moronically simple path: I was always in plays when I was a kid, doing community theatre, summer stock (semi-professional summer theatre season) and that sort of thing. Acting was just an extension of my social life, something that I got encouragement for and that I enjoyed doing. I never thought about it as a profession and I never saw it as my identity, but at the same time, I did not prepare for anything else. I was at university briefly – on a Bachelor of Fine Arts programme in Acting at the University of Wisconsin. The programme has evolved into a full professional programme since then, but at the time it was quite a mixed bag. I enjoyed being exposed to lots of different kinds of people and as it was a state university in one of Wisconsin's few metropolitan areas, many of the students came from working-class backgrounds. The professors in the theatre department were all into different techniques,

from classical to Grotowski-based psycho-physical work. I stayed at the school to encounter group techniques for a little while and then I joined a small non-profit theatre called Theatre X in Wisconsin.

If I have had any training, it has been training by doing; I simply performed a lot. Theatre X was a great company for me at the time because it was small and created its own work. Back then, I also enjoyed hanging out in small-press bookstores and reading about Jerzy Grotowski, Robert Wilson and Richard Foreman. At that stage, I imagined that at some point I would grow up, bag the experimental work and become a ham-bone actor, a working commercial theatre actor. Being an actor with Theatre X was tough because you do not make a lot of money and the collective environment breeds a lot of fighting and administrative headaches. I began to feel sick of being so marginal and I wanted to head for New York, because, back then, my idea of being an actor meant Broadway. Movies were a million miles away; I did not know anyone in the movies, I had no plans to move out to California and I was certainly not going to bang on doors. I loved movies, but I did not feel I had access to that world.

I arrived in New York City in 1977 with no money, lived in bad neighbourhoods and fell about two economic classes. I started to educate myself a bit, to make up for the fact that I never really got an education and began to look around at what was on Broadway and beyond. When I saw Elizabeth LeCompte's work, I made a beeline for The Wooster Group. I went over to The Performing Garage, where the group was based, and more or less said, 'I just want to be around you people.' I started working as a carpenter, did very small roles on stage and slowly I insinuated myself into the company.

What made you join The Wooster Group rather than going into the commercial theatre?
I had my hands full with The Wooster Group. It was a very complete life, I started liking the idea of being an artist and even started accepting the marginality of it.

You have played everyone from T. S. Eliot to the Son of God. You have run around on stage in a grass skirt with your penis painted green. Is there anything you would not do? What would prevent you from taking on a role and, on the other side of that question, what attracts you to a part?
It depends whether you are talking about theatre or film. In theatre,

with the exception of working with Richard Foreman and Jeff Weiss, I have never worked outside The Wooster Group in New York City. At The Wooster Group, we normally develop the pieces through a process of devising rather than working with a straight play. I do not choose a role; I choose partners with whom to make the work. Elizabeth assigns roles at The Wooster Group and the principal partners have been the same people for about twenty years.

Selecting roles is something I do for movies. I suppose I look for something that offers me possibilities, as I am not attracted to a role that I see very clearly. If I understand a role too fully right off, it feels as though the work is cut out for me and I prefer work that does not feel like work. In determining whether to take a role or not, I always look to the people I will be working with on a project. I need to feel some kind of a relationship – but not a complete relationship – with the character I am playing. It has to be a tease, a curiosity; it should be an invitation to learn something new or go some place you do not quite know. You have to have enough of a taste for the character that it seems organic and not ridiculously miscast. There is the seed of a relationship between the character and myself in all the roles I have played; all the characters are facets of myself. I am interested in the extent to which actors can transform themselves and how an actor is able to walk in somebody else's shoes and empathize with people who have experiences that are very different from their own.

What kinds of characters would you avoid?
The obvious ones.

How do you develop the extravagant characters in the pieces you do with The Wooster Group?
The larger-than-life Wooster Group characters are all created from a need to tell a story. I do not say, 'I want to play a chicken heart today.' They are all functional and you cannot apply traditional theatre criteria to them. It is not like saying, 'I want to play Hamlet.' Sometimes interviewers will ask me, 'There must be a role that you are dying to play?', but I come up blank every time because I do not think about roles like that. I would be suspicious if I did, because it would mean I was trying to serve my own agenda and if I were to do that, I would not feel invigorated by the role. I am no braver than the next guy, but I think that in order to enjoy what I do, I have to trick myself into situations that I feel

a little uncomfortable with, so that I have to work, fight or scam in order to succeed. In the case of The Wooster Group, I have a very strong director who sometimes puts me in those situations without me even asking. Take the examples of *North Atlantic* and *The Hairy Ape*, where Elizabeth made me speak so fast. Making me do this is totally perverse, because my natural speech rhythms are so slow.

Do you sometimes feel like a round pin in a square hole?
I always feel like that; that is the nature of living.

Do you have a definition of acting?
It is very flexible, because acting a role depends on what is required. What some people would call bad acting, I would not call bad acting at all. If you put certain movie stars in a play, they may not have the tools at their disposal to perform on stage without embarrassing themselves, yet they are fantastic in movies. The same applies to stage actors trying to make films. So how do you distinguish good acting from bad acting? It is all performing in one way or another. I like to think of it in terms of different acting for different kinds of performances, and some actors are clever enough to know what mode they have to be in, depending on the material.

Do you find it easy to switch from one mode to another?
I do, but even within the move from film to theatre, there are internal switches. I think different things are required each time, and every time you begin a new project you have to re-invent the process and what it is you do.

Would you describe the relationship between your theatre and film work as symbiotic?
In terms of the actual activity of performing, my theatre and film work feed each other constantly. At one level, acting for both stage and screen is all pretending. It is about dealing with obstacles, trying to find the truth, being loose and listening. There are enormous differences between theatre and film, but there are also great similarities. The difference is something akin to comparing a musician recording in a studio to someone performing live in a club. Basically, though, it is the same activity.

I think it is amazing how little crossover there is between theatre and film. The Wooster Group does ensemble work; the productions are never vehicles for me, although in the case of such shows as *The Hairy Ape*, my role was central to the production. If anyone wants to see a movie star or an idea of a person from the movies, they are not going to get it at a Wooster Group show. Conversely, some of The Wooster Group's core audience can be a little snobbish about movies.

Do you prefer working in film to theatre?
They do different things for me and I feel like I need them both. Whenever I go away from the theatre and do a film, I always feel like I am disturbing my work in the theatre, and whenever I am at the theatre for too long, I feel restless for my 'career' in film. Theatre is healthier in the respect that it is more of a spiritually invigorating medium. Its temporality is simultaneously the great thing and the horrible thing about it. Theatre is a living thing; it is flexible, mutable and you cannot hang on to it. It only lives in people's memories. When you have been in theatre for a long time, you feel like an alchemist, mixing things right on the spot.

I love working in film, but it is so mediated that the actor is just one of so many collaborators. Film is a director's and editor's medium, but socially film actors are more revered than theatre actors. Theatre is a very poor medium; you do not make any money and it is highly marginal. Broadway is supposed to have some kind of respectability, but if you have been in a Broadway theatre lately, you will know it is pretty tawdry and lacks vitality. I find our theatre company, The Wooster Group, very vital, but you cannot deny that it is also very marginal.

If I only worked in theatre, I would get a little bitter and feel small. I enjoy being pulled in two directions; film and theatre are worlds with different concerns, rewards, expectations and rules. To run backwards and forwards between the two forces me to examine what I really think about acting and to cultivate a beginner's mind about what I do for a living.

Does that mean you feel fulfilled, but often tired?
I sometimes feel fulfilled and sometimes feel tired. In some ways it is a lonely life because I do not feel part of either world: I am not so involved in the movies that I hang out with movie people, go to premières and parties or know other movie people; similarly, when I have been working in the theatre and then go off to do a movie, I feel displaced from the theatre world. It is an embarrassment of riches on the one hand, but on the other hand, my life is a little schizophrenic.

How does this duality work logistically?
Trying to organize my schedule is very difficult. I envy the people who are in the theatre all the time because they have a sense of uninterrupted continuity. When we sit down and discuss a piece, there are parts of the development that I do not know about because I was away doing a movie. That can be frustrating, but on the other hand, I get to have adventures and bring my experiences back to the theatre.

What are the skills you most value in actors you admire, and are there any particular actors who have exerted an influence upon you?
I admire stamina, grace and selflessness, and I do not like needy performers. The way in which some actors give themselves up to the material is usually a reflection of their intelligence and broad view of the world. They do not think the play or movie is about them; they have a wider agenda. I recently worked with the Chinese director Yim Ho on the film *Pavilion of Women* (2000). He was talking about Buddhist philosophy one day and very simply said to me, 'You American people that get into Eastern religion are always beating yourselves up about your ego, but there is nothing you can do about the ego. You need an ego to stay healthy and to be able to function, so your view of the world needs to get bigger and then proportionally your ego will get smaller.'

The things I admire most in an actor are intelligence, flexibility and compassion. The trouble is that everything in the theatre and movie industry conspires against that! They are businesses: they have to develop a product and sell it. You as an actor have to identify that product, solidify it, fix it, give it value and let people know they are lucky to be in the room with you. The reality is that you have got to balance the business side with giving the best performance. I am touched by performances that give over to the story and the language. Acting is not about size, restraint or understatement; it revolves around building a relationship with the movie or play.

There are very few actors whom I would hold up as a model consistently. You can admire their choices, or how they conduct their lives, but very few actors are consistently good. I like particular performances, but I do not look at a single career and say 'fantastic'. There are moments when you think Alan Arkin is the greatest actor in the world and then there are other times when you think Robert De Niro or Max von Sydow is great. Who knows . . .?

How do you prepare for a role?

It depends on how you feel. Sometimes you have to do a lot and some-times you do not have to do anything; it depends whether a character is very close to you. For me, you do whatever it takes to give you the authority to pretend; you do whatever makes you feel you have the right to be this person. Sometimes you need to do a lot of preparation to inform what it is you are trying to play. For example, once I played a boxer and obviously you would have to be an idiot not to realize that in order to play a boxer, you are going to have to learn how to box. A boxer uses their body in a particular way and that is the key to the character, or at least that is *a* key to the character.

I love acting for the adventures associated with it and because it pre-sents you with wonderful opportunities to get into somebody's head. I had a terrible education and I am forever a student now. It is great when your job frames an experience in such a way that you engage with something and take it in. If you are going to play a factory worker, for example, you might start hanging around at a factory. You start to get into the heads of the people working there and that is an exciting life experience which will definitely inform your choices when you play the character.

So you would actually prepare for that particular role by spending time in a factory?

If I thought it was important. For example, with *The Hairy Ape*, a play that takes place on board a ship, I chose to go back in the ring with my boxing trainer, rather than work on a ship. It was not about finding the mask for that character through their physical job; it was that my char-acter was more of a boxer than a worker and 'worker' was not an idea I could put my hands on. You need to play around to see whatever feels right. I do not think an actor's job is to interpret; an actor's job is to do the story and be the story.

How do you prepare a role when you are working in a devised piece where there isn't a play or a screenplay?

You have to wear a couple of hats. The Wooster Group is extraordinary in one way because the technicians, designers and actors are sometimes the same people and we are all in the rehearsal room together from day one. Sometimes we may get the set or costumes very early, and some-times we get them very late, but everyone is in the room working with the music, the text or whatever, together. The process is all about problem-solving, digesting material and making a relationship with it.

The material appears in lots of different ways. Sometimes we can be very conscious of why we are working with particular material, sometimes it can feel arbitrary and sometimes intuitive. My process is to show up, not get ahead of myself, cleanse myself of any expectation and try to figure out my interest in the material and my relationship with it. I find out what I like to do and why I am doing it. The problem is that the process is very difficult to talk about because you are inventing as you go along.

Do you find most of the ideas come from your interactions in rehearsal, or do some of them come when you are on your own?
It all happens in the space for me. Some of the other actors are much more conceptual than I am, but the emphasis for me is on doing it. The other thing about The Wooster Group is that we have a very full-on approach to rehearsal: we rehearse things as if we were going to perform them that evening. Rehearsing in this way often makes me feel like a failure, which is why I like performing better than rehearsing.

The Wooster Group often invites an audience in on the late stages of rehearsal, calling it a 'work in progress'. Do you think the goal of acting is performance? Is there a clear distinction for you between a work in progress and a performance?
The distinction is made when you realize you have got to the point where you do not want to work on the piece any more. We continue to rehearse a show even if we have been doing it for many years because Liz keeps changing things to keep stuff sharp. One of her greatest talents is that she does not become attached to what she makes; the second something stops living for her, she will destroy it or take it apart. There comes a point in the rehearsal process when you feel ready to show something. Sometimes we have to open a show for commercial reasons. International touring is our bread and butter and it is hard to take a 'work in progress' on tour, so any piece we do has got to be finished if we are going to tour it.

Performance is the goal of acting. Increasingly, as I get older, I have developed an aversion to people from the company coming up to me in the dressing room after a show, saying things like 'Hey, that was a great show' or 'Oh man, that really sucked'. There is a natural tendency to make judgements and I am trying to discipline myself not to, because an actor knows intuitively not to make the same mistake again and again. If you get too obsessive about your performance, it can strangle you.

I dislike rehearsal because it makes you realize that what you are doing just disappears into thin air. If there is an audience present and a greater formality to the proceedings, you feel like you have more control as an actor. One of the things I find difficult to deal with on occasion is the speed at which Liz works. Sometimes she will say, 'No, no, it's not working.' I will say, 'Come on, give me a second, let me try it again.'

'No, no, forget it,' she'll say. 'This is not a game and we are not giving out prizes. *It does not work*, so let's move on.' In a performance, you have more licence to play within the structure, but nevertheless, Elizabeth is there every night, sitting in the audience.

Why do you often have a visible prompter sitting at the front of the audience in your performances?
Even if I have done hundreds of shows and know my text perfectly, it is nice to have the outside person there. Similarly, it is part of The Wooster Group's aesthetic not to hide what goes into making a show. All the stuff that is normally hidden from view in most theatres, such as the lighting rig, the hydraulics and so on, are fully visible in a Wooster Group show.

What was your most challenging performance?
On principle, I cannot say because it always changes, so I will answer the question broadly. The most challenging role is the one where you feel as if you are failing; where you feel like you do not have it and you do not know where you go from there. You are off the track and you have to do something to get back on it, but at the same time you have to let it go. Acting is a wonderful combination of actively seeking something and at the same time letting it go. This is great training for life.

Apart from Elizabeth LeCompte, what other directors have you responded to most creatively?
I like almost all the directors I have worked with. You look for a director who gives you a good set-up. A mythology exists about the 'actor's director', a remnant of the Method ideal, where the director pulls the actor aside during the big emotional scene and manipulates them psy-

chologically so that they have that breakthrough moment and cry. That is not the way I experience the relationship with a good director. What matters to me is walking on to a beautiful set, with good actors and a good script, where the director tells you what has to be accomplished and gives you everything you need to accomplish it. I love an insightful director who knows how to put you in a situation or give you a good mask. When I think of good directing practice, I think of David Lynch in *Wild at Heart* giving my character those rotten teeth. It seems quite a simple idea, but the whole character was in those teeth. Initially, when I read the words 'he has yellow, stumpy teeth' in the screenplay, I would not have said, 'David, maybe we should get some full-plate dentures to change the way I talk and the shape of my mouth.' Maybe some actors would do that, but it did not occur to me. So when David said to me, 'We have got to get you to the dentist to get those dentures,' I thought, OK, and once I put those babies in, they gave me the whole character. That is the hallmark of a good director: someone who enables you to find that mask or tap into your imagination to really live in the text or actions.

Martin Scorsese is another example of a good director. His view of the world is so specific that you know what has to be accomplished, so you do not have to keep banging your head to find things.

In your movies, you tend to take on serious dramatic roles, but at The Wooster Group you often play madcap, comic characters. Would you ever consider doing comic roles on screen?
I would love to do comic roles on screen, but I just do not think people think of me that way; people do not think I am funny. Maybe I have not cultivated that side and perhaps part of me is lazy. I was once hired for a black comedy many years ago, but the movie got shut down. There is no point in doing a comedy for the sake of showing people that I can do a comedy. I would say that some things I do on screen *are* comic, such as my role in *Wild At Heart*. The character I play is a force of nature, the worst man in the world. There is this really beautiful scene where the character forcefully seduces a woman and when she submits to his advances, he says, 'Hey baby, I don't have time right now,' and just leaves her. The sexual politics are very twisted; he is grotesque but there is something beautiful about his badness. Unlike a lot of villains, the movie does not try to justify his behaviour.

Do you find the comic roles you have played on stage in any way easier than serious roles?
I think comic acting is more difficult, because of the timing factor.

Who do you find are the most useful critics of your acting?
Definitely not journalists. It goes without saying that I find the people I work with, such as my director and fellow actors, much more useful. I do not seek out criticism; it is what it is.

Do you ever read the critics?
I used to all the time because I thought it would be helpful to know the lie of the land, but I am starting to think about criticism in a negative way because you react to these people and it makes you self-conscious; even if the reviews are positive, you harden into an identity. If you do a movie and you read wonderful reviews about your performance, you start to cling to that as your identity and then you have something to protect which will make you less flexible and more likely to come out with a lot of 'I' statements such as 'I must', 'I should' and 'I am'. The same thing can happen with negative criticism; it can make you think, 'Oh the fuckers, they think I am terrible. I will show them.' You start reacting to something that has nothing to do with you. In theatre, criticism is deadly. If an actor reads a line about their performance such as 'There is this extraordinarily moving scene in the piece where the man strokes the woman's face and kisses her on the cheek', that moment is going to be ruined! Too much information is bad.

Do you go through certain processes before you go on stage on the night of a performance?
I practice asana, the physical component of yoga, every morning; I do breathing exercises and try to relax. Just before I go on stage, I have certain rituals that always change. I always tell myself to relax, be with what is, and get on with the show.

Does talking very fast, as you do in North Atlantic, *take special preparation?*
It is difficult for me to speak fast, so for this show, I run through my lines for the whole play as fast as I can before I go on stage. It takes me about twenty minutes to just reel off my dialogue and I know it well enough to just go straight through. I do that not just to get my mouth working, but also to get me in the rhythm of the show.

What are the most productive rehearsal conditions?
In theatre, I like good-humoured, relaxed rehearsals, with lots of doing and very little talking. In film, rehearsal is a good place to get to know the other performers, anticipate problems and difficulties in the schedule, and find out about a missing skill that you have to learn. In both theatre and film, it is hard to rehearse outside the context of the space or room; if you cannot rehearse in the actual space, it is pointless. If you rehearse too much in a different space, things get over-defined in the absence of the reality that you are going to be in.

What are your plans for the future?
My plan is to keep on doing what I am doing. I am ambitious and hard-working. I have always been suspicious of plans and I go cold when people talk about dreams because often you do not know what you want until you are there. I am not working towards a big goal, but I am motivated to go in a certain direction by all the little footsteps. I delight in little movements rather than the big picture; one step leads to the next, you gather momentum and before you know it, you are in motion. Sometimes I think this is the best thing about performing; I like it when you are conscious of the big picture but your attention is really right in the present. When you perform text very fast, you are with the text but always leaning towards the next thing. You cannot sit on anything because once you collect yourself, the words lose their energy, drop, and reflection and stagnation take over. I believe that you can reach out without knowing what lies ahead of you.

Eve Ensler

Eve Ensler is a playwright, activist and screenwriter. Her OBIE-Award-winning play *The Vagina Monologues* (1996), a series of monologues centring on the vagina as the locus of female experience, has been performed on Broadway both as a solo show by the playwright herself and by leading American actresses including Glenn Close, Calista Flockhart and Rosie Perez. The world tour of *The Vagina Monologues* initiated V-Day, a global movement to stop violence against women. Now in its fifth year, V-Day is celebrated on or around Valentine's Day, 14 February. Eve Ensler's plays include *The Depot, Floating Rhoda and the Glue Man, Extraordinary Measures, Ladies, Scooncat, Lemonade* (2000), *Necessary Targets, The Good Body* and *Conviction*. Ensler's play *Necessary Targets* (Villard Books, 2001) has had benefit performances on Broadway, at the National Theatre in Sarajevo and at the Kennedy Center, and opened in New York in 2000. She was a recipient of a Guggenheim Fellowship in Playwriting. At the time of interview, Ensler was midway through her run of *The Vagina Monologues* at off-Broadway's Westside Theatre.

Given that you are best known as a writer and have not had any formal acting training, what made you want to perform your play The Vagina Monologues?
I became very attached to the women I'd interviewed; I had a really deep desire to tell their stories and I felt it would be a good way of protecting the intimacy and sacredness of the interviews. It began as storytelling and then it evolved into a full-blown performance. In a way, I feel as though I approached this as a storyteller, not a performer. It has become more emotional and more integrated as I have gone along, and I feel as if I am actually performing, but without trying to.

How do you define performance, as opposed to storytelling?
I am not sure there is such a difference between storytelling and performance; it is all about what you set out to do. In the case of *The Vagina Monologues*, I do not see myself as an actress, having never really acted before; instead, I see myself as a writer, telling stories. As the months go

by, I have been getting more comfortable with doing the play on stage and it gradually feels safer to let myself go. I have been able to allow more and more of the women I interviewed into the process and that is what has evolved into the performance. Now, *The Vagina Monologues* is neither a public reading nor a writer telling stories. I am actually subsuming myself into other people and it feels like a performance.

A huge amount of research went in to writing The Vagina Monologues. *Was there any additional research you undertook to put the work on stage?*
No. The actual process of interviewing the women themselves greatly informed the piece: memories of their environments, their homes, their cafés, what they were wearing and who they were, accompany me on stage every night.

What do you do before you go on stage every night? Do you prepare mentally and physically in any way?
I have my little rituals and I am very, very superstitious. I had a particular song that I listened to before I went on every night; recently I changed it, but for five years I had to play the same song every single time before I performed. I listen to two songs as I warm up, but I do not know that I want to share all the rituals because they are private little things that help me get focused and thinking about the women. Then the whole crew, from the stage managers to the lighting people and myself, do a little circle: we have something or someone in particular that we are doing the show for every night and we use the opportunity to focus in. I always have some woman in mind that I do the show for every night, to keep things real and remind myself of why I am doing it. All this takes me about an hour, so I usually get to the theatre an hour before the show.

To what extent does the audience affect your performance?
Completely. Last night, for example, we had a very difficult audience who were very unforthcoming. They hardly laughed and did not seem responsive at all. Those performances are much harder for me, but when I feel that the audience is there, it is as if we are all on a wave. I just ride the wave. Shows like last night's make me feel like I really have to work hard and like I am on my own. I am aware of myself and I keep thinking, 'Oh, they bloody hate this' and 'What am I doing?' and 'This is torture'.

What do you do in those circumstances? Do you always think the audience is to blame? Do you try to alter something about your performance in any way?
I try everything, but I have now developed this theory about audiences; I believe an audience defines itself in the first three minutes and very rarely can you change it. There is a slim chance that a miracle will occur, but generally, within the first three minutes, you know the animal you are dealing with. Sometimes it is the greatest thing and sometimes it is hell, but the odd thing about the theatre is that usually on the nights when I have had the most wretched experience and I think everyone hated it, I hear people leaving the theatre going 'thrilling', 'fabulous'. It leaves me puzzled because I felt no connection.

What tells you how your audience is going to behave within the first three minutes?
It is to do with energy. *The Vagina Monologues* is like a journey. People either throw their bags willingly on the train and jump on board, or they drag their bags and do not want to leave home. There is a certain amount of relativity involved, though; people who I talked to today said they thought last night was a really responsive show, but the people who worked on the show knew what a dreadful night it was.

How have different audiences reacted to the show in different countries? Have you noticed any differences?
Not really; the response is pretty much the same everywhere I go. The Brits were a little shy at the beginning: they would not accept it at first, but they got going in the end. Audiences vary in every place every night, but the general receptivity has been very similar.

Do you enjoy seeing an ensemble cast perform the play? Or do you prefer doing it yourself?
When I perform the show, it's very grass-roots; the fact that I have been there gives it a certain authenticity. When different actresses do it, it becomes an event: a performance by a cast of well-known stars. Both ways are equally interesting and valid; I like to perform the piece but I am also thrilled about all these other people we have got lined up to take over. As a writer, I think that is fantastic. We have got Ricky Lake, Shirley Knight, Marisa Tomei, Gina Gershon, Alanis Morissette and Brooke Shields, to name just a few. It is a pretty amazing group.

Has your performance been inspired at all by seeing any of the other performers do it?

Not really, because I have not seen that many other people do it. As a matter of fact, I saw Gillian Anderson do the 'Vagina Workshop' monologue in London and I realized something very interesting about the piece: that people bring their own personality and character to it. I could never do the 'Vagina Workshop' the way Gillian Anderson does it and I am not supposed to. I find the different ways people do things so fascinating. Glenn Close did the 'Cunt' piece in New York in a completely different way from how Melanie Griffiths did it in London. They both worked in their own way.

Famous actresses have jumped on The Vagina Monologues *bandwagon to promote different causes – Glenn Close, for instance, recently said she was proud to be part of 'Eve's Army'. What do you think about using star-power on stage to promote different causes?*

In the 1960s and 1970s (and even the early 1980s), when we were on the streets, people really cared about social issues. In the late 1980s and early 1990s, everything changed, and the only way to get people to see anything now is through celebrities. Do I think it's a good thing? I think it is an unfortunate thing; it is sad that issues, ideas and circumstances do not in themselves move people. Part of me thinks that it is very generous of stars to use their power to get people thinking about causes. For a long time, I resisted going in that direction because I did not want to be part of celebrity culture, but one day when I was standing on the corner of 23rd Street and 7th Avenue in New York, handing out flyers, and people were basically spitting on me, I thought, 'This isn't working. People are not coming and they do not give a damn. I am not reaching anybody.' So I started to ask stars to do the work and people came; they signed up and got involved in the issues that I was concerned about.

As far as I am concerned, whatever it takes to get people to stop women from being raped or beaten, whatever it takes to stop wars, whatever it takes to spread the wealth, whatever it takes to create a different kind of reality, we have to do it. This is the form that meets these times; I do not know that it will last for ever, but I am very grateful to the stars for helping my cause.

What are the skills that you most admire in actors?

I love actors who are willing to be dangerous and who tell the truth.

This morning, I was at a rehearsal of another play of mine, *Lemonade*, which is about to be performed in New York. We were working on this scene where one character, a bulimic who survives for most of the play on a diet of cherries, has a breakdown and starts eating all this food with butter in it. We were struggling to figure out the scene, when I came up with the idea that the actress should eat a loaf of bread on stage. Now, I know this actress is obsessed about food, the way I am. I thought that asking her to do that on stage would throw her. But you know what? She jumped in, grabbed a loaf of French bread and shoved it down. That is what I admire: actors who know something is the scariest thing they could possibly be asked to do in the whole world, but they do it. The second thing I admire is people who are not afraid of passion. The theatre is a place of passion and it is great when actors are willing to go deeper and deeper into the duality, pain and beauty of it.

How has your work as a director and writer been affected by your experiences as a performer?
These days, I have so much more respect for performers than I have ever had in my life. Performing *The Vagina Monologues* has been the most thrilling, arduous and totally consuming experience I have ever had and I still have not realized the full magnitude of it. I have developed enormous respect for an actor's bravery and ability to get up on stage every night, no matter how they might feel, and I think I am much more sympathetic to actors now. In terms of being a writer, the experience has also taught me a lot about audiences: you have to keep a sense of the audience when you are writing. It is not that I am going to shape my work to cater to the audiences from now on, but I am now aware of the dance that happens between the audience and the performers on stage.

Has your work as a director or writer been affected by any other actors or styles of acting?
I often write with particular individuals in mind. There is a brilliant actor called James Lecesne for whom I have written a few shows. I know what his capabilities are and I know he can go places that a lot of other people cannot go. Thinking of him challenges me to go further as a writer, to push emotional boundaries and explore complex terrain. I like writing for Glenn Close, who is incredible: fierce, brave and willing to be everything. If I am writing for Glenn, it is really fantastic because I do not have to limit myself as a writer.

Do you see yourself tailoring the roles you write to suit particular actors?
I would not go so far as to say that I tailor what I write; tailoring implies limiting yourself. I would go fully into the character knowing what the actor's range and dimension is.

Describe the rehearsal process in terms of acting, directing and writing.
In terms of acting in *The Vagina Monologues*, my rehearsal process is literally just getting up on stage and doing it over and over again. I do not think I ever had a rehearsal process as such; I just did it for one group of people, then for another group, and so on. I would not even know how to rehearse.

I love watching rehearsals of plays I have written because I love the process of discovery. It is interesting to watch actors defining a word, finding an element of a character, or what a speech or scene is about. I think rehearsal is everything and I wish we had more rehearsal time in America than we do. I have worked with the wonderful actress Shirley Knight many times. Once she did a play of mine and it took her a long time to find her character. I learned from her that it takes a long time to find the play; the process is as intricate for the actor as it is for the writer. Both Shirley Knight and Joanne Woodward (who directed Shirley Knight in a play of mine) taught me so much about process, time, delicacy and moments when it is right to make a suggestion and times when making a suggestion would be really premature.

What is your favourite moment in rehearsal?
The best times are when the actor finds a defining moment, just like the incident with the bread I spoke of earlier. The speech had sounded didactic and the character was not at all likeable, but when she started eating bread, suddenly she was funny, weird and disturbing. The effect was very contradictory. We only had to try one thing and suddenly the moment was revealed.

Have your views of acting changed over the years and what are your views on the future of women in performance?
I hope people will stay in the theatre and I want the theatre to be a political, emotional, passionate and vibrant force. I want people to get their hands dirty and not to feel perfect and movie-star-like. The theatre should be the place where an actor becomes the people he or she might not meet in this life. It should be about inhabiting darkness and

inhabiting other aspects of the world. Theatre is a place of passion and frankly I think the world is becoming passionless. I think the internet, television and computers have virtually caused people to shut down on passion.

I particularly hope that women find the theatre. A lot of younger actresses who have been forced into film from the start of their careers have gotten really excited about *The Vagina Monologues* because they have not had any stage experience and they are really longing for it. If you do movies for a while, you end up asking yourself, 'What is this?' and 'Where is my life?' I don't think you can sustain your soul on movies.

Who would you say are the most useful critics of your work?
I look to other people in the theatre, close friends and other writers or directors for opinion and advice; the person I live with, Ariel Orr Jordan, is also very perceptive. He knows me and my work very well and can provide an ongoing frame of reference. I have a few close friends who are very critical and help me a great deal, but the newspaper critics rarely ever help me. I would love to live in a world where I felt that criticism was about the exploration of ideas, ideology or methodology; I so rarely feel that. I long to have someone looking at what I do with intellectual hunger.

Do you think you will ever go on stage again?
Yes, definitely. I got a little addicted to it, I must say. I am going to begin thinking about the new piece I am working on as a one-woman show. I love acting.

Danny Hoch

Danny Hoch is a New York-based actor best known for his solo shows *Some People* (1993) and *Jails, Hospitals and Hip-Hop* (1997), directed by Jo Bonney. Born in 1970 in the Bronx, New York, Hoch won an OBIE Award (off-Broadway Theatre Award) and a Fringe First Award at the Edinburgh Festival for *Some People* in 1994. The production was made into a television programme for HBO (Home Box Office – one of the USA's premier television networks). Hoch spent the first half of the 1990s bringing conflict-resolution-through-drama to adolescents in New York City's jails and alternative high schools with New York University's Creative Arts Team. He has written and acted for television and film, including HBO's *Subway Stories* (1997), Terrence Malick's *The Thin Red Line* (1998) and Fox Searchlight's *Whiteboys* (1999). Hoch is the recipient of a Solo Theater Fellowship from the National Endowment for the Arts, as well as a 1996 Sundance Writer's Fellowship. He was named a recipient of a 1998 CalArts/Alpert Award in Theater as well as a 1999 Tennessee Williams Fellow. *Jails, Hospitals and Hip-Hop* received a Bay Area Theatre Critics' Circle Award for Outstanding Solo Performance. In New York, the production received a 1998 Drama Desk Award nomination and was subsequently made into a film.

How would you define acting for theatre and for film?
I do not think you can define acting for theatre and acting for film without first defining theatre. The origins of theatre lie in the ancient traditions of African, American, Asian and European theatre, and the original purpose of theatre was not solely for entertainment. Today, acting for theatre and film is mostly about entertainment, but in ancient times, people acted for religious, educational, entertainment and historical reasons all combined into one. These elements were not compartmentalized, the way we tend to compartmentalize theatre or film acting today. Depending on what the context is, acting for theatre is an ancient social event. Acting for film is a contemporary *a*social event. The social event in film is supposed to happen when people gather in a movie theatre to watch the finished product, but acting for

film is a contrived, hyper-compartmentalized, ultra-asocial, fabricated event. It is very boring, but in most cases it pays a lot of money.

How does acting in Jails, Hospitals and Hip-Hop *the film compare to acting in* Jails, Hospitals and Hip-Hop *the play?*
The film of *Jails, Hospitals and Hip-Hop* is a mathematical experience. Everything is plotted out in scenes, and then there is a shot list and a storyboard. You have to shoot it from angles and make sure you get the reverse angles. When you are making a film, you are not engaging in a social event. When you act, you should feel possessed, but it is hard, coming from a theatre background, to become possessed in the mathematical context of film-making.

What was your training as an actor? Do you specialize in a particular acting technique?
I had a formal actor's training: I trained at The High School of the Performing Arts in New York City and followed this traditional acting training with a period at a conservatory. I dropped out and winded up studying in London at BADA (British American Drama Academy). I have studied every technique, from Suzuki and Meisner to Stanislavsky and Boleslavsky, but one technique that I did not study during my formal training but which greatly interests me now is ancient theatre technique. It is important to know about Stanislavsky's ideas so that you can be your own dramaturg. However, learning to act through such a tradition can be very unhelpful, especially to an American, because it is so mathematical. Many of the European techniques inherited by American acting schools were created in a socialist context and America is the antithesis to that. When we Americans try to perceive these traditions, we do so very mathematically, because we do not subscribe to the world that they were created in.

We have no tradition in the States because we are too young. We have nothing technique-wise that compares to the history of Russian, Japanese or African theatre. America is an amalgamation of many cultures and traditions and we carry these traditions with us, whether we like it or not, even as we assimilate into whatever American culture is. What I seek in a technique is something that combines the context of all those traditions, because that is what America really is; a combined context of people's histories, cultures, behaviours and languages.

How do you go about acquiring this combined context for your acting? Is it something you develop over time by coming into contact with all these different traditions?

I do workshops with young people all the time. Occasionally I am asked to do a college theatre class and the last thing I want to talk to the students about is technique. I want to talk about politics and the social responsibilities of being an actor. I am interested in thinking of the actor in terms of a blue-collar worker. This is something that a lot of American theatre programmes do not stress, with their interest in getting your big break and becoming a star. The way acting is taught and thought of in this country has very little to do with what is happening in society. We carry the opinion that as actors we are enlightened entertainers and that people will be bettered by coming to our shows. This attitude stresses administering instead of incorporating, and it is a big mistake.

Why do you act?

I act because people should do what they are good at; it is something I can do and it is my responsibility to do it. It is also my responsibility to do it in a socialist context. The majority of actors in this country act within the capitalist context and the balance needs to be addressed. We may never achieve socialism in this country, but if we have some inkling as to what is going on in this society, then as artists it is our responsibility to respond to it. That means engaging in community theatre. Generally, people in America perceive community theatre as renditions of *Oklahoma* at the local church, but I think of what I do as community theatre. This kid walked up to me after my show in Berkeley, California, and he said, 'Wow, I never thought of coming in here because I thought they only did community theatre, but I really liked your show.' I replied, 'My show is community theatre, it's just for a different community. It is for a community that has been excluded from theatre for so long; a younger community of many colours.'

Since the inception of this country, theatre has been primarily for white folks and rich folks, but my community is dominated neither by rich folks nor white folks. I think I am doing community theatre in the ancient sense, in trying to get young people to come to my shows. Once a kid came up to me after a show, saying he was from my neighbourhood and that he had never seen anything like my show. He said, 'You had me laughing, but you really got me thinking about some stuff. I am going to bring my friends.' Then he said, 'Say, when are you going to be on Broadway?' and I said 'What do you mean?' He was like, 'Look where you are. You should be on Broadway.' And I was like, 'Man, you can't even afford Broadway. You don't want me on Broadway. Your neighbourhood isn't invited to Broadway.' It is absurd that being on Broadway or in a film is valued so highly in this country, as if the only communities that count are the ones whose stories are being told in Broadway shows.

Do you not see a role for yourself as a 'democratizing force' of Broadway?
I would like to see myself that way. I think there should be a revolution: the people of New York City should take over Broadway and kick everyone else out because theatre is supposed to be for the people. Broadway and off-Broadway are not for us; there are ten million people in the city and the majority of us live in Brooklyn, the Bronx, Upper and Lower Manhattan and Queens. Yet the shows on Broadway in New York are about riverboats in Mississippi and the audiences that come to see the shows are also from Mississippi. Off-Broadway theatre is no better, with its stories about struggling suburban upper-middle-class families, playing to an audience also from the suburbs. Why don't they show those plays out in the suburbs? Why don't the Mississippi people have their Mississippi plays in Mississippi? Then, when we have a theatre festival, we can all exchange our shows and see how great everything is, but it is sexist, racist, classist and every other -ist there is for these kinds of shows to dominate our theatres in New York City.

What are the skills you most value in actors you admire? Which actors have exerted the strongest influence on you?
One of the most amazing actors I have ever seen is the American actor Roger Guenveur Smith. I strive for the relationship he creates with the audience. It is an uncomfortable relationship, while at the same time he educates them and makes them laugh. Another really good actor is the solo theatre artist Dale Orlandersmith. She is a heavy-set black woman with long braids, yet she transforms into any character you can possibly think of, from twenty-year-old skinny Italian men to eighty-year-old Jewish men and thirty-year-old white women. I also think the actress Rhodessa Jones is phenomenal; I find her theatre very moving.

How have you developed your acting skills?

I think I have developed my acting skills to their limit. I do not go to acting class, but I do feel challenged by roles all the time, and I like to think that if I take on a challenging role, my skills will somehow be honed.

How comfortable do you feel taking on roles created by other people?
I feel comfortable and I look forward to it. It is lonely being a solo actor. I am looking forward to shooting my next film, in which I have a meaty role and get to work with other actors. The last time I was in a play with a cast of actors was three years ago.

If someone asked you to play a Shakespearean hero, for example, would you turn it down, or would it depend on the context?
I used to love doing classic plays, whether Shakespearean, Jacobean, Restoration or whatever. It was once my dream to play Hamlet on a British stage. Doing Thomas Middleton's *Women Beware Women* at London's Royal Court Theatre as part of my acting programme made me question why I was an actor. Although the classics are timely and universal, these days I do not think I would jump at the idea of doing Shakespeare. The American obsession with the classics is a mistake, leading us to ignore the contemporary stories of our own society that are desperately waiting to be told.

There is a wonderful socio-political theatre group called Culture Clash, comprising three Chicano actors from California who tour around different cities telling a story about that city. They have performed a story about Miami in Miami, about LA in LA and about the New York Latino community in New York. Their work could loosely be described as political-sketch comedy, and you should have seen their last show, *Radio Mambo: Culture Clash Invades Miami* (1994). In that show, they played about fifty different characters from every ethnicity in Miami. To me, that is American theatre. We need to get over our Shakespeare-and-classics obsession; it is a dysfunction worthy of psychotherapy.

How much research do you undertake for a show?
Not much. When you read about actors saying, 'I studied the character, I prepared the role . . .', it sounds like such a mathematical approach to acting, whereas I am interested in the visceral approach. I try not to research characters; I listen and observe people, but I consider this to be

habitual rather than research. Some people think an actor should absorb everything around them, noting how people move and so on, but to me, it is instinctual. Some of my characters have taken a year to develop, some of them have taken a day and some have taken half an hour. The characters come from a visceral place and not an intellectual place. I do not create a particular character to be a paraplegic, have a speech disorder or whatever; the character tells me. When people ask me how I come up with my characters and whether they are based on real people, my answer is that each of my characters is a facet of myself, combined with about five people that I have met, known or heard. All of the characters in my shows had been brewing for a while, not on a tape recorder, a notepad or in my head, but as a concoction of the instinctual actor. I am always listening, but I never think while I am listening, 'Oh, that would make a good character.'

How do you prepare mentally and physically for a performance?
My routine keeps changing. I do not smoke and I do not drink around performance time. I am a vegetarian these days, but for several years I was vegan in and around the months when I was performing because dairy products are not good for the throat. Eventually this changed because I had to feed my soul with pizza. Technically, I do not eat any spicy foods around performance time and recently I learned that the acids from tomatoes or chillies, vitamin C pills and citrus products eat away at your vocal cords while you are on stage. For an eight o'clock show, I do not eat after one-thirty in the afternoon, although I drink a lot of water. I do warm-ups before every show that vary from night to night: a combination of callisthenics, yoga, break dancing, salsa and rituals. Some nights I meditate and I break dance, while other nights I do the *New York Times* crossword puzzle and sip tea. I always do a particular ritual before every show, involving certain instruments and items from my altar.

What are rehearsals like for you? How did you work with your director, Jo Bonney, on your last two shows?
Rehearsal is very strange for an actor who writes his own work. Officially, I am not a playwright or dramaturg, so I cannot watch a video of myself and say 'This is or isn't working, textually or stage-wise', because you cannot re-create a stage event with a mechanical device. Jo Bonney, who is a dramaturg as well as a director, came on tour with me to all the

cities in which I workshopped the show. *Jails, Hospitals and Hip-Hop* toured twelve different US cities before it opened in New York, and I still do not think we are done with it. In every city, Jo would sit in the audience and give me notes afterwards. Through Jo, I have come to think of the role of the dramaturg as not necessarily being about literary texts in and of themselves; dramaturgy is about finding the relationship between the actors and audience and whether a text serves the social event. Jo is one of the few directors with an eye for that relationship. For her, directing is not just about seeing if something looks good on stage, but asking if we are achieving the social event of theatre. Jo challenges me both as a writer and as an actor, and working with her is not about me standing there looking at a script, it is about her saying, 'Look at the script in your head, change these things around and then tell me why.' She is priceless in terms of helping me figure out my own process.

When there is an idea in your head, how long down the line do you have to go before you know you have got a show?
I am usually running late preparing a show in time for performance. For example, we had five weeks in Berkeley, California to workshop a show, five nights a week in front of audiences. When we got to Berkeley, I had fifteen characters but only three of them had been sketched out on paper, so we just tried stuff out in front of the audiences and by the end of five weeks we knew what the characters were and what the order was. I had to show up every night and deliver a performance, knowing I was winging it and yet knowing that people were out there expecting it to be great. It was nerve-racking and I got ill from the stress of having to go out there and be vulnerable every night.

What are the most productive rehearsal conditions?
Getting out in front of the audience. Part of my rehearsal process takes place on stage in front of an audience, but if I am not in front of an audience, I like to have a space with a window.

Talk about your experiences with audiences. How do you feel when you are performing in front of a young crowd of people who rarely if ever have been to the theatre before?
Recently I gave two of my best performances. One was a performance of *Jails, Hospitals and Hip-Hop* in a jail on Riker's Island in front of 250 inmates who were between eighteen and thirty. Some of my characters'

stories are based on Riker's Island, making it an ideal setting. Performing in front of prison inmates was nothing new for me, but this time it was amazing because it felt like ancient theatre; not only did the audience respond to every nuance on a literal level, but I was re-enacting their daily experience on stage. Catharsis is an understatement; it was tremendous!

The other amazing experience I had recently was at the University of Michigan, again with *Jails, Hospitals and Hip-Hop*. The guy who organized the show made sure that people under thirty dominated the 700-strong audience, so I was presented with the cross-section of Michigan society, from Latino students to African American and Asian students. There were tons of Asian, Latino and African kids in the audience; it was definitely not the normal picture people associate with Michigan. These kids were so amped to see the show, because they were used to being dragged by their teachers to see Shakespeare, or rap versions of Shakespeare. The kids went crazy. I heard the same stuff after the show that I heard from kids in New York. 'What do you call this?' they asked me. When I said 'theatre' they didn't believe me because they were not used to theatre being about them.

These are my favourite relationships with audiences. My least favourite relationships are when I am in a regional theatre and the audience is over sixty, white and suburban. Some of them get it and need to come to my show, but a lot of them are expecting theatre with a British accent because their understanding of theatre is Shakespeare, Beckett or Spalding Gray. I had an old lady come up to me after my show in New York one day. 'I like your work,' she said, 'but why are you playing these foul-mouthed characters? Why don't you play, say, a British character? I'm sure you could do that really well.' Of course I can do that, but why should I? We are not British here, although some of us want to be. I have had people walk out of my show at the Public Theater in New York, saying, 'He's not speaking English. I want my money back. This is not theatre.'

Barb Jungr

Barb Jungr, singer, writer and performer, was born in Rochdale and grew up in Stockport, south of Manchester, England. In the late 1970s, she formed a band called The Three Courgettes, which performed new-wave versions of gospel classics and was discovered by Island Records. She worked for many years on the alternative cabaret circuit with the guitarist Michael Parker in the duo Jungr and Parker and toured all over the world. Jungr's themed shows have toured nationally and internationally and include *Hell Bent Heaven Bound* (1991), *Money the Final Frontier* (1992), *Songs from the Heart* (1995), *Killing Me Softly* (1996), *Red Roses Blue Ladies* (1997), *Sex, Religion and Politics* (1998), *Bare* (1999) and *Chanson, The Space in Between* (2000). She regularly leads workshops on her performance methods and her work as a teacher, performer, broadcaster and writer has taken her all over the world; she has toured Sudan, Cameroon, Malawi, Burma, Yemen and Tanzania for the British Council.

What was your training as a performer?
I didn't have a formal training as such. I wanted to be an actor when I was young, but my life didn't take me directly down that road – it was music which brought me to theatre. I began performing at my convent school and though I didn't have a conventionally 'cultured' education (my teachers, for example, wouldn't have known much about Harold Pinter), there was a passion for popular performance and we did a Gilbert and Sullivan opera every year. I learned classical violin, wrote the school play nearly every year and was the class clown. My childhood was full of music, singing and performance: my parents took me to opera, pantomimes and variety plays, and my father is Czech and my mother German, so I unconsciously absorbed artistic influences from their backgrounds. My favourite bands were groups like The Who, who had a tremendous sense of theatricality, and Tamla Motown and Stax – also very theatrical.

I went on to do a degree in botany at Leeds University. I kept up the music and singing, and moved to London immediately afterwards to avoid being pushed into taking a research degree. I did session singing and applied to join bands. I was then lucky enough to be involved in playwright Pam Gems's first hit *Dusa Fish Stas and Vi* (1976), so from the very first I had a sense that theatre and music belonged together. For a time I managed a punk band and became interested in the presentation of punk, which linked a very particular kind of anarchic performance with music. I describe myself as 'schooled', not trained, and my first schooling was in gospel music with a band I formed called The Three Courgettes with Michael Parker and Jerry Kreeger. We were heavily influenced by gospel music sung by groups like the Golden Gate Quartet, Swan Silvertones and Dixie Hummingbirds from the 1940s, and we sat for hours analysing their songs in great depth, working out the extraordinary blends of rhythm, harmony and syncopation. We busked in the King's Road and Portobello Market in the late 1970s, got a recording contract and progressed to clubs and the touring circuit.

You performed on the alternative cabaret circuit. Could you describe what that was?

In Britain in the late 1970s and early 1980s, there was an explosion of tiny clubs in which people did all manner of acts. Like the 1920s cabaret acts in Weimar, artists such as Alexei Sayle did storytelling, mime, stand-up, musical numbers, skits and character sketches; you worked solo or in duos or trios. Physically, vocally and politically, you went on stage and had to get your point across to an audience who had not necessarily come to see your act. I did cabaret with Michael Parker for thirteen years, in some periods for six nights a week, so I was constantly constructing material, inventing stage personas, acting and singing. For a time, Michael and I switched to the folk circuit, a dinosaur throwback, where it was acceptable to turn up in your gardening clothes and tell appalling jokes: I'd been used to sharp political thinking from cabaret where it was important to be non-racist, non-sexist and have some understanding of global politics. The cabaret circuit has now turned into the stand-up comedy circuit and is dominated by boys talking about sex – hardly politically radical.

You're known especially for your themed shows. Could you describe what they are?

I construct material round a theme: for example, *Hell Bent Heaven Bound* (1991), with Christine Collister, Michael Parker and Ian Shaw, was a show that celebrated death and was driven by the question of why death is a taboo in our society: all the songs and all the spoken material were about death and investigated it from many different angles. I frame the shows with a running subtext, and there is always a political point. They are a form of musical theatre and I stage them in theatrical ways, using lights and costume to create certain effects. *Hell Bent Heaven Bound* won a Perrier Award at the Edinburgh Festival and hit a tremendous chord with audiences. I wanted to push the bounds of fringe theatre, so I worked on a show called *Brown Blues* (1987) with comedian Arnold Brown, where we experimented with mixing stand-up comedy and music. My stage persona was rather apologetic, Arnold played the outcast and Michael Parker said nothing at all and simply played guitar brilliantly, which was a fascinating combination. Arnold was at the height of his comic genius and it was an enormous privilege to work with someone of his calibre. In *Money the Final Frontier*, all the songs were about money and the subtext explored the interconnection of art and money. It toured extensively, especially in Canada, but I realized that I needed to extend myself in other ways. I began to do themed solo pieces accompanied by piano, and wrote and performed *Songs from the Heart* (1995), *Killing Me Softly* (1996) and *Red Roses Blue Ladies* (1997). *Songs from the Heart* was about the anatomy of a relationship, and *Killing Me Softly* was based on my aunt, who was murdered. I linked the material in ways which really forced the audience to work on the connections and meanings. It was a hard show to perform, but audiences went through extremes of emotion, laughing and crying during the course of the evening. The solo shows toured nationally and internationally, and that was the point when I began to be asked to lead workshops on my performance style. My personal belief is that everyone has creative potential and, given the appropriate space, can do much more than their usual constraints allow. My workshop style is pretty much to get people to allow themselves to find out exactly what they can do, and get them to do it. It amazes me what people have shown in them once they're given a chance to show it. They come because they want to explore something for themselves, not because I have a magic technique or formula. Basically, I just make a space for them and they do the rest.

How do you create a stage persona?
I think of creating a persona as adopting a mask and speaking through it. I recently played a mad Master of Ceremonies for a performance piece with the Amici dance company. I worked as I always work – by

experimenting in front of a mirror, by finding the right make-up and the right physical characteristics, then exploring movement. I don't work naturalistically, I work with grotesque elements and characteristics that are larger than life. My theatrical influences come from cabaret, film and music hall; part Doris Day, part Liza Minelli, part Edith Piaf and part Vesta Tilley.

What sorts of performance have influenced you?
I'm interested in the voice work of Paul Newham, who was himself inspired by Roy Hart, and find Grotowski's concept of physical theatre exciting. In my own shows, I want people to feel deeply, to undergo some sort of cathartic process. It's only since I completed a Masters degree in ethnomusicology (anthropology of music and world musicology) that I've acquired a technical vocabulary for performance. I've come to understand that my work has considerable parallels with European cabaret and that I am a *chansonnier* – the text and narrative of song are vital to me. But the Masters also schooled me in African and American music and performance techniques and I am equally fascinated by Persian tribal singing and performance as I am by Malawan choral performance. Newham allowed me to access vocal timbres. Ethnomusicology gave me a language through which to access information and thoughts on music – I had to get my brain in gear for the course. In the work that I was privileged to be part of in Africa, I found faith again in the power of music, ritual, dance and theatre to completely transform everyone involved. It restored my faith in the power of performance, which I'd lost. In Africa, performance is central to tribal cultures.

How do you understand your work as a chansonnier?
The tradition of the chanson comes from France, and the *chansonnier* explores the space between clear and complex emotion, often, for example, the space between love and rejection. For me, the voice is all about transcendence. I have no interest in exploring old songs in their original style and I commission translations which are contemporary. *Chansons* are text-driven and theatrical; Greco said that singing a *chanson* is like singing a one-act play and that you must be in the service of that play. The most famous *chansonniers* are Jacques Brel, Edith Piaf, Leo Ferre, Jacques Prevert, Marguerite Monod and Charles Aznavour. I have developed my singing of chansons into more than a musical event

and, apart from my own physical performance, use slides of paintings that were painted especially for the songs by artist Garry Laybourn, whose work explores the colours of emotions. They can be enjoyed as simple pictures but they have a more complex relationship to the rest of the material in the performance.

Can you explain your remark that voice is about transcendence?
All good art is about transcendence; good art takes you beyond the everyday and mentally transports you somewhere else. I find singing for myself compelling to do and absolutely cathartic, and I observe catharsis in others when I am teaching. In many African tribes, the purpose of singing is to contact the spirits, and gospel is about expressing yourself to God. In the West, we have lost the connection to the fundamental point of art: expression and celebration. Instead, art has become consumed by capitalist conceptions of entertainment and is about money-making. Singing can release voice and body, and I've seen transformations in people time and time again.

What do you want to achieve with your performances?
I want to move people with my performance work, but I also want to effect a change in my spectators and make them think about the society in which we live. I want them to have experienced an enjoyable, moving and meaningful show, and to carry on reflecting on what they have seen and heard after it is all over.

What are your ambitions as a performer?
I want to take my work round the world. I've travelled a great deal, but acquire more and more of a taste for it. I want to play all the wonderful festivals; there's a whole series of them around the Arctic Circle that you can play in the summer and you get the midnight sun. I'm working on a new show with dramaturg, director and writer Noël Greig, and on a collection of Persian and Anglo music for a concert with Persian tribal singer Parvin Cox. I'd like to extend my acting even further, and keep trying out new ideas. Learning is about doing, and I want to make as much work as I can while I'm still here, because you never know how long you've got.

Luba Kadison

Born in 1906 in Kovno, Lithuania, Luba Kadison was a founding member of the renowned Yiddish theatre company, the Vilna Troupe. She performed in the original production of Solomon Ansky's *The Dybbuk* (1920, Warsaw) and played the lead role of Leah throughout her years on the stage. She married the actor Joseph Buloff in 1924 and came to New York with him in 1927 to join Maurice Schwartz's Yiddish Art Theater. When Buloff began performing on Broadway and in Hollywood, Kadison continued acting with Schwartz in New York. In a career spanning several decades and many countries, she performed in I. B. Singer's *The Brothers Ashkenazi* (1938, New York), played Stella Adler's love interest in Sholom Asch's *God of Vengeance* (1928, New York) and won great acclaim for such roles as *Anna Karenina* (late 1950s, Buenos Aires) and Linda in Arthur Miller's *Death of a Salesman* (1951, Brooklyn). The Buloff–Kadison Archives are at Harvard University, which also published their memoirs, *On Stage, Off Stage: Memories of a Lifetime in the Yiddish Theater* (Harvard University Press, 1992) and Buloff's novel based on his childhood in Vilna, *From the Old Marketplace* (Harvard University Press, 1991).

How did you come to be an actor?
The theatre was my cradle and it has been with me all my life. I grew up with the Vilna Troupe, a Yiddish-speaking Jewish theatre company directed by my father. Theatre was a hobby to my father; professionally, he worked as a painter. I was a kid of seven or eight in 1914 when the war broke out and we were forced to leave our home town. Our lives changed within the space of twenty-four hours; we did not know where to go, so we found ourselves in the town of Vilna, the Lithuanian capital, and quickly had to find a place to live.

One day in 1916, two young Jewish actors came to my father with a proposal because they had heard that he had directed some wonderful productions with his troupe of amateur actors. Vilna was under German occupation, but the Germans of 1916 were not like the Germans of 1945; there were Jewish officers amongst them, including German writers like Stefan Zweig and Hermann Struck. The actors told my father that they wanted a Yiddish theatre company in Vilna to meet the demands of the large Yiddish-speaking population. The Germans were fighting the Russians and did not want to promote the Russian language, so a Yiddish theatre seemed like a reasonable idea, given the similarity between the Yiddish and German languages.

My father was delighted to accept the offer; the company was established in 1916 and became world famous. I started to play such parts as little boys and little girls in my father's productions when I was a girl. Acting on stage was as natural as drinking a glass of water to me; I was brought up to it. Our idealistic young company would rehearse plays in our apartment. We went through some very hard times because there was hunger in Vilna; frequently we had nothing to eat, but somehow my mother would find some potatoes and give one to each actor so that they could go on rehearsing.

The theatre company was built on Stanislavsky's model, with plays performed in a realistic style and a repertoire that consisted of Jewish and Russian works and plays from the world repertoire. We did not strictly follow Stanislavsky's system, but we saw Stanislavsky as a model for good realistic theatre. Melodrama still prevailed as the acting style of the era, but we were interested in realism, purity and acting.

When I was thirteen, a new actor joined the company: his name was Joseph Buloff, and he was very talented. I married him at the age of seventeen. The company started touring around the world and I performed roles in the plays for many years until I moved behind the scenes and helped out on productions. My last stage appearance was in 1968, as the Witch in *A Chekhov Sketch Book* (1968, Buenos Aires). I stopped performing because I felt that I was getting too old for the parts I played, and the parts for older female actors did not appeal to me. I enjoyed being an assistant director to Joe and he needed my help.

We were brought to America by the impresario Maurice Schwartz, who was at that time the director of the Yiddish Art Theater in New York. Coming to the States was a very lucky break; it saved us from the Holocaust and the concentration camps. However, we only spent a couple of years with Maurice Schwartz. My husband, who was then directing the troupe, began to develop a modern, expressionistic style, but New York was becoming too commercial and the new style did not go down well with the mass audience. That is not to say New York was not a good theatre city; there were many fine actors there and the standards were high, but we were young and very idealistic. So we left New York and went to Chicago, where we did Yiddish-language adaptations of classical works from around the world, such as Tolstoy and Molière. The work was great, but financially we were in bad shape.

How did you learn your acting skills?
I learned to act by being in Vilna productions. One of the plays we performed was *The Dybbuk*, by Solomon Ansky. I think *The Dybbuk* is the greatest Jewish play and perhaps one of the greatest plays ever written. With its cabalistic atmosphere, my father thought the play needed special insight from a director, so he engaged the services of David Hermann, a director with a cabalistic and Hasidic background, to stage the world première. I was fourteen at the time and played a little part in the production, which premièred in Warsaw in 1920. Hermann took me aside one day and told me I had potential but that I needed training. There was no Jewish drama school for me to attend in Vilna, but because I spoke good Polish, Hermann advised me to apply to a very good drama school in Warsaw. So, one day when we were in Warsaw touring *The Dybbuk* in 1920, I summoned up all my chutzpah and turned up at the Polish acting school and told the administrator at the school that there was no Jewish acting school in Lithuania and that I wanted to be a Jewish actress. She looked at me with my curly hair and Jewish eyes and asked me what I could do. I read her the two poems I had prepared and somehow impressed her, so I was offered a place. I learned a great deal in that school and stayed for two years (1920–2). I had two wonderful teachers; one for speech and scene work and the other for movement. The teachers said I possessed a magic quality and a lovely voice when I played the role of Medea.

During those years, I went to school during the day and performed in the theatre at night. Poland was very anti-semitic at the time, but nevertheless I would still receive the occasional compliment from Polish audience members. One evening, however, I was very upset when a woman came up to me after a performance and told me to get back to Palestine. I realized at that moment that Poland was no place for me. That night, I put on my galoshes and walked through the wintry streets of Warsaw alone, reciting Polish poems and feeling very sad. Eventually I decided it was time to return home to the Vilna troupe and soon felt fine again.

Do you think acting can be taught or is it purely instinctual?
I believe very much in using your instincts as an actor and that a person is born 'to be or not to be' an actor. You can develop acting skills, but the real spark has to be in you from the start. Being with other actors, working on your art, is a school in itself and you develop your skills as an actor through ensemble work, dialogue, connection and communication. The body is also very important, which is why television and movies are a completely different art from the theatre. In theatre, you can talk with your body as much as with words, whereas in the movies, physicality is less important. Discipline and work are also essential to developing your skills as an actor, and many people waste their talent.

How would you approach a text?
In the Vilna Troupe, the text would mostly remain in the hands of the director; scripts were not handed out to actors. The director would tell us what play we would be performing and would explain it to us; then we would explore the play with action. As little kids, we were taught by our father to sit down and write out the parts by hand, which we would give to the actors. Each actor would have his own lines and cues because we did not have the facilities to print a whole script for each actor. One production we did was an adaptation of *Anna Karenina* that toured to Argentina, with me in the title role. It was quite a task adapting a text like that to suit our audience, especially since we had to compete with a popular film version of the novel starring Greta Garbo that was playing in cinemas at that time. After seeing the movie, I was scared stiff about playing the part. At night, I read and re-read the novel and thought very hard about it and in rehearsals I developed a feeling for the part and began to love the character. One day, in rehearsal, I overheard one actor tell another actor 'Luba will never make it'. I went home that night and cried, and decided to push myself harder. It was hard work but I got there in the end and the show was a great success.

What is the relationship between the actor and the troupe?
I believe in ensemble theatre. Acting is not a part-time business; it should be a part of everyday life. A company should be like an orchestra; all the greatest companies have a sense of ensemble.

How do different international audiences affect you?
Generally, audiences would be drawn to the theatres around the world

specifically to see us. In places like Buenos Aires, we had a lot of people who did not understand Yiddish, but they found something new in us despite the language barrier. We attracted a young audience but we did not reach out to the masses; in general, the audiences who came to see us knew about us already. It felt like the performers and audiences were all part of one family and the level of communication was great. Israel became our second home and we used to travel there for about six months a year. Jewish actors are scattered all over the world. When you bring them together with a good director, the audience really feels the connection. However, we did not always get a fantastic reception everywhere we went. In New York, for instance, our theatre jarred with most people's commercial tastes.

What sorts of parts have you been most drawn to?
I have a leaning towards parts that require deep feeling and emotions. I love playing Leah in *The Dybbuk*, Anna Karenina and anything by Eugene O'Neill, who I believe is one of the greatest playwrights. I also enjoy comic roles, such as in plays by Molière and the folk Jewish writer Peretz Hirschbein, who portrayed his Jewish characters as country people in such works as *Green Fields* and *A Secluded Nook*. The best parts for actors are found in the ensemble repertory. An ensemble actor is like a musician: he can play Mozart, Beethoven or Chopin equally well, and can give you comedy one night and tragedy the next with equal skill.

Are there any types of parts you would refuse to do?
I had a couple of seasons in which I was forced to play in musical shows. They were done in a melodramatic style and I did them because I needed the money.

What was your most challenging performance?
We once did a benefit performance for a famous actor who was sick. I played the part of Leah in *The Dybbuk*; I was feeling a bit depressed and I really did not want to go on, but I told myself I had to rise above it. I was in a bad state that night but I will never forget the performance I gave. There are a number of occasions in an actor's career when something happens and he or she gives an exceptional performance; that was one of those nights.

How do you prepare to go on stage?
I get butterflies like everyone else on the day of a performance. In the wings, I get a little nervous, but when I am up on stage, I just get on with it. I believe in craft; English actors are so good because they have more craft than any other actors in the world. The essence of craft is timing, because when you are in a bad mood or things are not going right in your life, craft helps you get through a performance and stand on your own two feet. If you do not have the discipline of craft, you can sometimes give a very bad performance.

Is craft something that can be learned?
It is hard to say, because in many ways it is instinctual. Craft makes you surer of yourself; it is a back-up tool. It gives you stability, like a master carpenter making a table.

Did you only ever perform in Yiddish?
Yes, only in Yiddish, though my husband sometimes performed in English on Broadway in such shows as *My Sister Eileen*, *The Whole World Over* and *Oklahoma*; and in Hollywood, in *Somebody Up There Likes Me* with Paul Newman, *Silk Stockings* with Peter Lorre and *They Met in Argentina* with Maureen O'Hara.

How did you find performing in Yiddish in America?
Persecuted Jewish immigrants came to America from all over the world. They worked hard all day in sweat-shops and lived in bad conditions. It was a hard life for them and the theatre was their main outlet for entertainment. There were many actors in the Hebrew Actors' Union and melodramas and musicals dominated the stages in New York. We were not interested in doing melodramas and musicals, so it was hard for us to find an audience for our work. We had our own aesthetic goals, so we decided to pursue them in other parts of the world.

What was it like playing a part like Linda Loman in Death of a Salesman *in Yiddish?*
The production was conceived in Buenos Aires with another actress in the role of Linda because I had decided to stay in New York at that time to look after my daughter during high school. When the New York producers heard about the show's success in Buenos Aires, they wanted to put it on in Brooklyn with me in the role of Linda. At first I thought I

was a little too sophisticated for the part, but the producers insisted, so I took it on. I was not sure how to approach it, but it grew to become one of my favourite roles. You cannot get too deep with a character like Linda; she has a wonderful kindness and common sense. Arthur Miller came to see a performance in Brooklyn in 1951 and liked it very much. An article soon appeared in a New York paper, joking that our company had returned the play to its Yiddish original!

Which directors have you found most inspiring in your life?
My late husband, Joseph Buloff, was tremendously inspiring because we had the same attitude, taste, understanding and background. He would let actors do the best they could and never force anything upon an actor; he would give all his actors freedom whilst creating a sense of unity. He was like a conductor in front of an orchestra and the American director Harold Clurman said my husband was one of the greatest theatre-makers in the world. We lived together for sixty years and he died in 1985. I never had trouble with any directors. I acted under Maurice Schwartz, who was not bad; he used to leave me alone to get on with my part.

What are your hopes for the future of acting?
Acting has turned towards the movies and television, and in general, theatre is struggling. Young actors all over the world have to fight very hard for work and act for free because they love it so much. Since the Holocaust, Yiddish theatre has died out because people have grown away from the language. Israel has a very strong Jewish theatre tradition, but most of it is performed in Hebrew these days. There is very little good Jewish theatre left in the world today and not much good theatre around in general. Despite the recent renaissance of interest in Yiddish theatre, people play around with it, and it is not really alive as an art form. As far as Yiddish culture is concerned, the true renaissance is happening in the realm of Yiddish literature, with the global popularity of such writers as Isaac Bashevis Singer and Sholom Aleichem.

Who are the most useful critics of your work?
I am! Whenever the curtain falls, I always think I could do better next time.

William H. Macy

Born in Florida in 1950, William H. Macy came to acting by way of the American Bethany and Goddard Colleges. At the latter school, Macy studied under playwright David Mamet, with whom he has been frequently associated throughout his career. After college, Macy, his writing partner Steven Schachter and Mamet founded the St Nicholas Theater Company in Chicago, where Macy originated roles in several of Mamet's plays, including Bobby in *American Buffalo* (1973), and Lang in *The Water Engine* (1976). In 1978, Macy left the company and went to New York, where he became a founding member of the Atlantic Theater Company with Mamet in 1985 and acted in numerous Broadway and off-Broadway shows, including the Tony Award-winning production of *Our Town* on Broadway (1989), the original productions of *Baby with the Bathwater* (1983), *Bodies, Rest and Motion* (1985) and Mamet's *Prairie du Chien* (1986) and *Oleanna* (1991). In addition, he worked in television and began doing feature films. His leading screen roles include *Oleanna* (1994), *Fargo* (1996), for which he garnered a Best Supporting Actor Oscar nomination, *Wag the Dog* (1997), *Air Force One* (1997), *Boogie Nights* (1997), *Pleasantelevisionille* (1998), *Mystery Men* (1999), *Magnolia* (1999) and *State and Main* (2001).

You have recently performed American Buffalo *in London and you are in the middle of performing the same show in New York. How would you compare acting in Britain and the USA?*
People used to think that British actors were more technical and American actors more organic, but that is not the case any more. We have all melded into one. Whether our techniques are the same or not, I feel we are all shooting at the same target. Because of the movies, there is now a general consensus as to what constitutes great acting.

What is the goal of acting?
I like an actor with a clear goal, who works towards an objective and does not care if a role makes him attractive or not. I like acting that is clean and unadorned, and I personally prefer it if it is a little on the unemotional side, just because generally I find emotionality tiresome. I

like brave performances, when people step out there and take a chance; even if it goes wrong, it is thrilling to see someone working without a safety net. I like acting that is organic and improvisatory, a performance that feels like it has been made up on the spot. I hate mannered performances that look like they were made up at home and brought in. I hate overly emotional performances, exposition and indicating. By indicating, I mean the elements that an actor puts into his or her performance to help the audience understand the scene, i.e. 'I hate this guy', or 'It smells in here', or 'I am a shallow person'. It is not the actor's job to make a scene anything in particular; it's an actor's job to find his or her action and tell the truth moment to moment.

Your feelings about acting sound very different from Stanislavsky-derived ideas about acting that have been so popular in the USA for much of the twentieth century, such as the Method.

No, what I am saying does not contradict Stanislavsky completely. There are two sides to Stanislavsky: one is all about physical action and objective and the other is about the emotional life of the character. The part that I think does not work and never has worked is all the emotional stuff, because everybody knows that you cannot control your emotions. If we could control our emotions, there would be no need for therapy, so any technique based on controlling emotions is just plain false. Artists want to tap into their emotions because that is where the truth lies. The emotions lie within the subconscious, therefore a technique should allow our subconscious to come forth unhindered and unpremeditated. I think actors should put their attention on what they want – on the objective – and let the emotions take care of themselves. If you are free and brave, the emotions will flow freely.

Everybody knows that if an actor wants the audience to cry, he or she must not cry, and if an actor wants the audience to laugh, he or she must not laugh. If you are doing a highly turbulent scene and it's making you feel all emotional, put a lid on it, get the job done and the audience will fall apart. The audience is smart and they can tell when you are manufacturing tears. They don't want to see you manufacture something, they want to see you *do* something.

That sounds like Practical Esthetics, the technique you have been closely involved in developing. Tell us a little bit more about this technique: how did it develop and do you find it universally helpful for all the kinds of roles you do?

If you have a technique that does not work on every style of performance, then you have no technique. Any technique must be absolutely adaptable. The development of Practical Esthetics began with David Mamet and grew out of his study of Sanford Meisner's technique that stresses the objective. Mamet refined Meisner by demonstrating the difference between what the *character* wants – the character's objective – and what the *actor* wants – the actor's objective.

The character's objective is based on imaginary circumstances. For instance, the character might be trying to save the kingdom, but you as an actor cannot save the kingdom because there is no kingdom and you are not the king. Thus the technique helps the actor to define and analyse the character's objective in such a way as to be able to do it on stage. You have to do something on stage that is real and concrete, with a beginning and an end. You must be able to accomplish your objective. It is not possible to persuade someone to 'save the kingdom', because how would you know when you had succeeded? It is possible, however, to do something like talk someone into 'doing the right thing'. This is an action I can test: I can see it in your eyes when you capitulate and I will know when I have gotten you to 'do the right thing', 'take a chance', 'admit your fault' or 'back my play'. These are all things I can actually do on stage, and I will know when I have accomplished them. What the character is doing and what the actor is doing are different things, but the audience cannot tell the difference. They do not know that I am trying to get you to 'do the right thing' because to them it looks like I am trying to get you to 'save the kingdom'.

Mamet also says there is no such thing, for our purposes, as a character. Character is a myth, a trick that we theatre-makers play along with the help of the audience. If you put me on a throne, dress me up and give me lofty speeches, then I am the king. What is the difference between the king and I? Nothing. Do I have to figure out how the king walks? That is absurd because I will never know how a king walks. Do I have to figure out what the king would think? There is no way I could know that. I cannot know what anybody would think and it is not important.

The audience just wants to accept the play, so tell them who is the king and get on with telling the story. Mamet says that the only thing an audience wants to know is what happens next. The audience does not care about the lighting, the acting and, to a large extent, the writing. When all of those things are brilliant and add to the through-line, then that is a boon, but that is not what they came to see. They came to be told a story and that is all that anybody wants. It is the actor's job to tell that story. In a way, Practical Esthetics is the next generation of the Stanislavsky system. Stanislavsky started the whole thing and he deserves all the credit for changing what was once a made-up art form into one that is based on science.

You seem to be talking about moment-to-moment work rather than the big picture.

The actor's currency is the moment. When Mamet first started teaching acting, he made us read *The Myth of Sisyphus* because the actor's job, like Sisyphus's, is never finished. Like Sisyphus, you have to roll the stone up that hill again and again. It is great to live in the moment as an actor, but the moment is fleeting. The muse descends upon you and you want to savour the moment, but you have to let it go and move on to the next thing. The same thing goes for when you screw something up; you desperately want to take another shot at it, but you have to give it up and live for right now.

Acting is a very frightening way to earn a living, in all candour. Human beings do not operate very well when they are afraid and one of the things that makes us fearful is the unknown. We try to control the unknown to abate that fear. We have routine, we try to pre-empt all the things that might go wrong, and attempt to control them as much as we can. An actor cannot do that; not only do we have to live with the unknown, we have to embrace it. You might be scared to death, but no one gives a damn; you have to get out there and do it anyway. Being an actor is learning to live with that fear.

How much research do you do to prepare a role?

You do what is required, but you must never confuse the externals of a character with acting. You may be playing a character with a hunched back, a limp or a lisp, but those things are not acting; they are externals. Of course, there is a big difference between people who do externals well and those who do them poorly. To a large extent, I think those things must be learned in the same way as you might learn to juggle or play guitar: accents, dialects, limps and so on develop through muscle memory. If you are playing a surgeon, there is a certain way you have to scrub up and handle the instruments. You have got to know all that stuff to bring whatever degree of verisimilitude you need to the role, but it isn't acting.

The truth of the matter is that every single thing you need for acting is right there on the page. Some members of the theatre community believe that a play is a puzzle that needs to be solved. Mamet is famous for saying 'It isn't a puzzle! I am not trying to trick you! I want this play to be a success! I have given you all the information you need.' If I needed to know what is outside the door, down the hallway to the left, the playwright would have told me. We have to trust the writer; if the information is not given in the play text, it can't be important.

What happens when there are elements in a play that are so archaic or foreign that you don't immediately understand them?
I think you have to do whatever homework is required to figure out what the phrases mean, as you have to understand what you are saying. The Brits do Shakespeare like it is second nature, but when we Americans try it, the words just do not fit into our mouths properly. There are so many words that the verbal gymnastics trip us up and it takes a lot of practice and experience to pull it off.

However, it is important not to confuse linguistic dexterity with acting. When you act properly, the words do not matter. Ideally, a pair of actors on a stage engage in a constant stream of improvisation: they follow the blocking they always do and say the words they always say, but the words do not mean anything until they ascribe meaning to them and they cannot ascribe meaning to them until one of them sees what the other is going to throw at them. If I want you to loan me fifty bucks and I see a stony face, I had better think of something to do that is going to soften you up. By the same token, if I look at you and you are looking all kind and sweet, then I do not need to take the same approach.

David Mamet gave me not only my technique, but also my aesthetic. He wrote a wonderful book called *Three Uses of the Knife* (1998). I found his equation of the actor's journey with the hero's journey in this book so moving; it made me feel heroic to be an actor. Mamet says our best heroes are not the superheroes who slay the dragon; with their muscles and brawn, of course they will win. Our favourite heroes are in fact the last guys we would send from the village to slay the dragon, and we vicariously fall for the guy who stares into the dragon's lair, scared to death. He knows he must walk in there and he has no idea how he is going to slay the dragon, but he figures out what to do and when he finally manages to kill the dragon, our hearts soar like eagles.

Every time an actor goes up on stage, they have to slay the dragon. I walk on stage every night with no idea of how to slay the dragon, or perhaps I have a good idea but I cannot be certain it will work, I do not know what the other actors or the audience are going to be like and there's the burrito I ate for dinner that's doing funny things to my stomach. There are just too many variables, so if you have the bravery to throw out all preconceptions and improvise from moment to moment on stage, you will feel like you are on the hero's journey.

What kinds of roles are you attracted to?
I seem to be good at taking the loser's role. I am not very good at hiding what I am feeling, so these types of roles make me accessible to an audience. It is very easy for an actor to give up, but I do not give up. If you are playing a loser and you know in the next ten pages you are going to lose, you must not anticipate the loss. If you start playing that loser ten pages in advance, the character is going to be singularly un-fun to watch.

Loser characters like the ones you played in Fargo *or* Magnolia *are also fighters. They keep going along their track and never give up, even though things are falling apart every step of the way.*
I love those characters and I would love to do a romantic comedy with a character like that. The baby-boomer generation is now in its fifties, and I think it would be great to do a romantic comedy about normal guys of my age, with balding heads and big bellies. I am just a normal-looking guy and most parts on stage and screen are for really comely-looking people. The rest of us get left out in the cold, actor-wise.

Can you talk about your own background?
I went to a little school in Vermont called Goddard College, from which Mamet had just graduated and recently returned as a teaching fellow. He started an acting class and out of that class we started a group called the St Nicholas Theater in the college. My friend and writing partner Steven Schachter and I re-formed the company in Chicago with Mamet. We did a lot of his plays and were wildly successful through the 1970s. The first play we did was *American Buffalo*, in which I took the role of Bobby. Alongside acting, I taught and wrote a play called *Mattress* (1975) and did a serialized musical for kids called *Captain Marbles* (1974–6).

The Practical Esthetics technique has evolved by casting away everything that does not really affect your action on the stage. Back in the

1970s, I played *at* the character: I would undertake character research, like carrying a fake wallet on stage with fake IDs. I used to write down what happened before the play began and knew what was outside the door and down the hallway. I did a lot of plays, about three or four a year, and from sheer laziness the research became sketchier and sketchier. I would do less and less of my homework, while at the same time I was teaching my students to fill their wallets with fake IDs. One day, the hypocrisy got the better of me and I asked myself what would happen if I left the wallet and fake IDs behind for one performance. The answer was that nothing happened; the fake driver's licence in my wallet made no difference to my performance.

It occurred to me a couple of years ago that so much of your attention is taken up with the technical demands of the play. Since so many plays have such short runs, you never get completely comfortable with the lines. You have to be careful not to paraphrase, you have to listen to cues, watch the blocking, be aware of the audience and be in the moment. Taking the attention off yourself and really concentrating on the other person takes energy and time, and there is so little left over for anything else. There is no time on stage to remind yourself of what your objective is. It is too late. If you do not know the objective by the time you get on stage, it is not going to work.

To my mind, there are two common mistakes that are made in rehearsing a play. The first one is how to learn the lines: you cannot act when you are memorizing the lines. If you try to act whilst memorizing lines, you inculcate line readings into yourself, so it is better to learn line readings by rote in monotone. Treat them as though they are gibberish, ascribe no meaning to them and memorize them as a technical exercise. You have got to be able to say them loud, fast, forwards and backwards. Never act them till you get on stage and you are looking at another person. The second thing is the purpose of rehearsal: the only purpose of rehearsal is to create habits. It is so busy up on stage that what you do up there you must do *habitually*. The rehearsal process should create the habit of the objective, so the first thing you should rehearse is the objective, or, in other words, getting another actor on stage to do what you want them to do.

Describe your ideal rehearsal conditions.
I can best answer that by telling a story. I was in charge of the schools programme at the Atlantic Theater in New York. We had lots of

students, so we decided to do five one-act plays. I chose my play, a little romantic comedy, and the other four directors chose theirs. The other directors picked all the bright, good-looking students and, being in charge of the programme, I got the leftover students. I picked the most unlikely person in the group to be the hero. In our first rehearsal, we sat around a table, analysed the play and decided what all the objectives were. In the second rehearsal, we did the same. In the third, fourth and fifth rehearsals, we did yet more of the same: practising the objectives in every way we could.

We had a total of three weeks to rehearse and in the second week we were still sitting at the table. Meanwhile, the other groups were already up on their feet and rehearsing. I could see that my group wanted to get up, but we continued to study our objectives at the table. In our third week, we were still sitting at the table and by now the kids were freaking. On the first day of the final week they started leaping out of their chairs as they were acting and I decided it was a good time to start blocking. They knew their objectives so well that I literally blocked the play in two hours. All I had to do was start them off, as it was clear where everybody had to go. It was a piece of cake because the play was living in them.

We decided to watch all the plays together, so the students could see each other's work. The other three groups performed brilliantly, but my play was boring and slow. It plodded along and people kept giving us encouraging remarks like 'That's sweet' and 'It's going to be good'. The next night, there was an invited dress rehearsal. That night, the other three plays fell apart, trying to repeat what they had done in the private preview performance the night before. My play was boring and slow, but it was also a little bit better. We spent some time trying to patch all the plays up. The other groups were in a state of panic. We did our second preview and the other plays were a total disaster, but my play was just a little bit better again; in fact, it was kind of good that night. Then we did our first public performance. The other plays were boring and shaky, but my play was sweet and well performed. The unlikely kid who played the hero suddenly looked kind of cute.

This is a longwinded way of saying I rehearsed the fundamentals first and they learned how to play the play when it got to the day. I am prouder of that production than almost anything else I have done. The playwright, who had done the play on Broadway, came to see it and said, 'Where did you find these people? We spent six months trying to find a cast. These guys are perfect!'

Our tendency on the first day of rehearsal is to jump straight into what we are going to perform. A lot of directors want to see you *perform* in the audition. They want to see you there, ready to rock, because they do not know how to direct a play, they do not trust themselves and they are afraid that if you get into trouble, they won't be able to help you.

How do you find working in film as opposed to theatre?
In the best of all possible worlds, making film is the same as making theatre, albeit in a truncated form. In the theatre, you can pretty much learn your lines in the three or four weeks of rehearsal, but I find that hard these days because I am fifty years old and I just cannot learn them that fast. In a movie, you have to learn the lines on the spot, but because it is usually only a page or so, you just need to develop short-term recall. Then the process is just the same, the only difference being that they are going to start filming through your rehearsals. In film, theatricality is not required in great amounts. Film requires realism and smallness because you do not have to play to an audience. Stanislavsky said, 'Play well, play badly, but play truthfully.' The same principle holds true for film as for theatre: do not make stuff up or overstep your stride. If you do not know what you are doing, just say the lines.

Do you feel as comfortable making films as you do theatre?
I am almost as comfortable in movies as on stage, but I belong on stage.

Who are the most useful critics of your acting?
My wife, Felicity Huffman, who is also an actress, is a great watchdog of my work. She tells me when I am not trying hard enough or when I am being cheesy. It is hard to get feedback from Mamet, but when you do, it is pretty good. It helps that I am good at script analysis; perhaps it is the director in me, but I am pretty good at figuring out what is really going on in a play.

Do you ever read newspaper critics?
I read them all. It is a bit like playing with snakes: I love it when I get good notices and it hurts when they are bad, but I read them anyway; I think there is something to be learned from them, whatever their view. I have just finished performing *American Buffalo* in London and reading reviews is even more educational there. There are so many critics in London, so you can get a thorough consensus on your work. It is tough

(69)

in New York; there are so few papers and the *New York Times* is so powerful that it is hard not to play to it.

The toughest thing about being an actor is feeling powerless. When it comes to the food chain, we are down there with the plankton. We cannot make a play successful, clear or beautiful; our responsibilities are so limited. It is very frustrating not to be able to give the other actors or the director notes. I have always thought that you can say something once to a director and if it is really important you can say it twice. If it is one of those life-and-death situations, you can say it three times; but in the end, you have got to do what he or she says.

The actors, more than anyone else in the industry, become celebrities. Don't you think that is a strange fate for 'plankton'?
Yes it is. The process can go horribly awry when an actor becomes bigger than the producer or director and starts throwing his or her weight around. When that happens, it makes everyone miserable. I believe in structure. We have got to hold the producer's feet to the fire when some actor is misbehaving; the producer must step in and get them to stop. The producer has got to be brave enough to say, 'If you do not learn the lines, I am going to fire you.' If the actor does not learn the lines, keeps showing up late or keeps costing the production time and money, the producer needs the guts to say 'I will see you in court.'

What motivates you to act?
Acting is how I make my living and I have done it enough for the sheen to have worn off a little. I have stuck with it through some very grim times because I truly like that moment when the lights go up or the camera starts rolling and it is just me and the other actors living in imaginary circumstances. I feel more comfortable in this situation than any other in my life. It is the one time when I feel invulnerable, brave and in control. Given what I have been saying, it sounds odd to say 'in control', but whatever happens, I am driving the bus. That joy has made it possible for me to persevere when perhaps a wiser person would have found a different profession. I know some actors who do not like being up on stage. They love the life, they love the theatre and they love acting in general, but in their heart of hearts, when the lights go up and everyone is staring at them and expecting them to come up with the goods, they do not like it. They get angry with the critics and audience. They have a bad relationship with that kind of pressure and lead tortured lives.

Given that so much of what you have been talking about is to do with reacting off another person on stage, how do you deal with monologues?
First of all, when you are doing a monologue, you are still speaking to someone. It could be a brick wall, but the brick wall changes because of the way the mind works. The audience listens to every monologue; the audience has a spirit, breath and life and it changes constantly. Sometimes it is possible to speak the lines to the ether. In some of Shakespeare's monologues, for example, you are laying out a problem to the world. You lay it out verbally and it allows you to look at it with some perspective.

Which is the director you most enjoy working with?
It is hard to say who is my favourite director. I loved working with Joel and Ethan Coen. Gary Ross was great, as were Paul Thomas Anderson, Mamet and Steven Schachter. A director must get everything in on time and I get mad with directors who are still running around into the twelfth hour of shooting. Unless there has been a meltdown, I am inclined to think the director did not schedule their day well. It is a director's job to lead the troops, to make sure we are on the same page and speaking the same language. A director should state the play's theme and make sure everybody sticks to that theme. It is a director's job to make sure that team spirit is good. To a certain extent, it is a director's job to say the unpleasant things to the actors, like you have got to work harder or you are not credible. It is difficult for an actor to see the whole picture. If you are doing your job well as an actor, you are in love with your character, but the director is the one who can see the big picture. He or she is the person who makes sure that the writer's story gets told.

What do you do just before you go on stage?
Generally speaking, I have to warm up my voice because I have blown it out a couple of times. It takes me about half an hour to do this and if I do not, I pay the price. Then I stretch out and get myself ready to go physically. I have a little routine; I fart around with the other actors. The rest of the warm-up depends what you have got to do when you are on stage. In *American Buffalo*, I have to come on steaming mad in the first scene, so to prepare for this I shadow-box. It is a very Grotowski solution to the problem, but the shadow-boxing puts me in a feisty mood. The whole warm-up process takes about forty-five minutes to an hour in all.

Do you have any broad aspirations for the future of acting?
I think things are improving. The quality of acting is getting better and audiences are smarter. I would like to see cleaner, simpler acting. The future belongs to the writers who do not include exposition in their plays; audiences are too smart for that stuff. I think jobbing actors should get a bigger cut of the money, especially in theatre. I wish all three unions [SAG, the Screen Actors' Guild; AFTRA, American Federation of Television and Radio Artists; and Equity] would combine and use their muscle to make sure that actors everywhere get better treatment.

Miriam Margolyes

Miriam Margolyes studied English with F. R. Leavis at the University of Cambridge. She has enjoyed a diverse acting career on stage, radio, in film and television. Her theatre credits include *Cloud Nine* (1979) and *Gertrude Stein and a Companion* (1985), which won her a Fringe First Award and a nomination for Best Actress in Australia in 1987. She appeared with Vanessa Redgrave in Peter Hall's production of *Orpheus Descending* (1989) and she has taken her one-woman show, *Dickens's Women* (1991), all over the world. In 2001 she appeared in *Romeo and Juliet*, directed by Peter Hall. Her role as Flora Finching in the film *Little Dorrit* won her an LA Critics' Circle Award for Best Supporting Actress and took her to America. Film credits include *I Love You to Death*, *Pacific Heights*, *Roadside Prophets*, *Dead Again*, *The Age of Innocence*, *Babe*, *House!*, *Not Afraid*, *Not Afraid* and *The Butcher's Wife*. Her television credits include *Girls of Slender Means* (BAFTA Best Actress Nomination), *The Glittering Prizes*, *The History Man*, *Blackadder*, *Cold Comfort Farm*, *Poor Little Rich Girl*, *Oliver Twist!* and *Tonight at 8.30*.

What was your training as an actor?
I had no formal training in the sense of attending drama school. From about ten or eleven years old I had elocution lessons, and at sixteen I was the youngest person ever to have completed the London Guildhall School of Music and Drama examinations. I didn't join an amateur dramatic club, instead I travelled round England with my parents and participated in music festivals and public-speaking competitions. I was really pushed along by my mother, who was very proud of my talents; I had tremendous fun and I think that's when I acquired a taste for being a winner.

In 1960, I went to Newnham College, Cambridge and studied English. I acted in and directed about twenty productions. I was a member of the University comedy club, the Footlights, and acted with John Cleese and Humphrey Barclay – it wasn't always the fun that you might imagine; women comics were more of a rarity in the early sixties.

When did you first perform professionally?
It's interesting that my professional career began in radio, through a

producer called John Bridges who knew me and got me an audition. I became a member of the BBC Drama Repertory Company and that's where I really got the chance to develop my skills, working with first-class actors. I've always maintained my radio-drama career, it's been a very important part of my life, it's where I honed my vocal skills, and I was fortunate enough to work with a wide range of artists such as John Osborne, Paul Scofield, Claire Bloom and Vivien Merchant. After that, I worked in repertory theatre.

Do you undertake much research for your roles?
You can never do too much research. Take my show, *Dickens's Women*: I studied Charles Dickens's novels at Cambridge and developed a life-long fascination with his work. I co-wrote the play with Sonia Fraser, who was also the director. All my reading of Dickens's books over the years and all my thinking about the characters went into the show. I did extensive period research: not just the historical and political facts, but the social history of the time, the social mores and expectations. I also researched the language of the time, the words that were used and the ways in which sentiments were expressed. For *Vanity Fair* (1998), I read up on social history: as an actor, I find that the more I know about the social values of a particular time, the more I can enter into that character's world and make the imaginative step of thinking myself into their world. I was in the original Joint Stock production of Caryl Churchill's *Cloud Nine* at the Royal Court, for which the whole cast were expected to read about the colonial history of Africa, and we brought our discussions into the shaping of our roles. I once played a catatonic schizophrenic and, in order to get a sense of what their situation might be, I sat in on case commentaries at Guy's Hospital and met sufferers. I think it is essential for actors to understand as much as possible about the characters they are playing; acting is about creating people and the best acting explores all dimensions.

How do you find your way into a character?
When I read a script for the first time, I have a blurry, indistinct image of the character. I see her standing at a distance, but the picture is out of focus. I first try to find the voice and am told that I change physically even as I speak, though I am not aware of it. I don't consciously think: how does this person walk? I try to think the character's thoughts. This probably sounds rather abstract and I have often wondered what actu-

ally happens during the creation of a character because my descriptions must seem mysterious to others. As I learn lines and think myself further into the character, I find that their image becomes sharper and aspects of me turn into them. At the point where my self merges with the image of the other and I am no longer simply myself, I have created the character. The interplay between actors on stage is also critical: to some extent, your character is also made by other members of the cast; it's an exciting experience when you feel your character growing in response to demands from others – in those situations, it's as though a baton is being passed from actor to actor. Of course, the audience also informs your presentation of a character, but the audience should never lead the actor, they should never be in charge of you. I refer to audiences affectionately as 'my lovely blobs' and audiences certainly show you things about a moment, a scene or a character that you might have missed; they may laugh unexpectedly, or fail to laugh, or react with silent intensity, and their responses can be very enlightening.

Are you conscious of any particular influences on your acting?
I'm not aware of actors who have influenced me directly. I admire precision, control and a spareness of presentation: 'the less, the more' sums up my thinking. I admired Flora Robson for her exactitude and Nigel Anthony for his verbal precision. A text should be spoken without any additional signpost to the audience and all actors have to discover verbal habits which can clutter a speech; extra 'ohs' and 'ahs' can muddy up what you are trying to say. A clean, uncluttered performance is a difficult thing to achieve, but Steve Buscemi, Johnny Depp and Edward Norton regularly find the spareness I'm talking about. Recently, I've been bowled over by Russell Crowe's ability to represent his screen characters with such clarity, and I thought Mel Gibson's portrayal of Hamlet found a simplicity and truthfulness that was very moving. I think it's best to be 'small' in acting. Temperamentally, I have an inclination towards the florid and can easily overact: directors frequently say 'Less, Miriam! Much less!'

What for you are the best rehearsal conditions?
I love rehearsals; it's thrilling to see everything come together. I am nervous of dropping the book, so I try to learn everything in advance. I remember a rehearsal of Tennessee Williams's *Orpheus Descending* (1989) which was one of the most exciting experiences I've ever had:

Vanessa Redgrave, an extraordinary artist anyway, gave a completely unmannered performance. The magic of it shone. It was one of the greatest performances I've ever seen and she didn't hit that level again once the production opened, but the fact that she could hit it all was breathtaking to me. Experiences like that are rare but all the more precious because they happen so infrequently.

Badly run rehearsals can be frightening and shocking experiences. I recall a production of Brecht's *Man is Man* which was the director's first professional work – he was used to nine weeks of rehearsal at Oxford University, not the three or four weeks in professional theatre. For days, I was asked to try one accent after another, as though this might be the key to the play. I was the only woman in the company and felt decidedly persecuted. Eventually I called a company meeting and said to the cast: 'You're all as bad as you think I am and we open in five days.' We asked for another director and got our wish, but when things go that wrong, it's the actors who are wholly exposed and who have to live with the consequences.

Peter Hall is a pre-eminently intellectual director and a joy to work with. As an actor, I need the intellectual structure of a production to be created for me and Peter achieves this in a way which is exciting and confidence boosting. Max Stafford-Clark is also interesting to work with. I learned a technique from him that I find useful when I'm having difficulty with a character; and it came out of his direction: 'Play the opposite of what you think you should be doing.' I found this a useful instruction because a character has more than one dimension – in fact, has a whole range of notes – and this opened a way of exploring depth. If I am hitting the same note, I now experiment with playing the character in a totally different way, to see if I release new energy. Max also works with Stanislavskian approaches to text, breaking it down into objectives, and exploring characters through verbs. I often find myself analysing a sentence, paragraph or scene in the same way, asking myself what I am doing and thinking it through with simple statements like 'I conceal' or 'I entreat' or 'I lust'. Generally, adjectives are poisonous in the theatre: 'I am distant' is far less powerful and precise than 'I reject' or 'I disdain'. Often a good director is someone who knows how to break a block in an actor. I remember Julie Covington had difficulty with a particular speech in *Cloud Nine*; Max told her to sing it and the passage made sense to her straight away. That wasn't a method as such, it was inspiration, and directors also need plenty of that.

Do you think you need different acting techniques for film and theatre?
I'm probably revealing myself terribly, but I think a lot of rubbish is talked about this. The scale may be different, but I don't ask the cameraman what the frame is, how near or far the focus is. I still have to be as real, as truthful as possible, whether the spectator is close or not, present or not, whether the focus is entirely on me or not. The truthfulness of an actor's performance is no different on film. I do find that I am far more dependent on a film director to lead me to the right performance, and will be completely led. On stage, I can judge the pitch of my performance and know whether I am getting it right but I find it difficult to be critically introspective on a film set and am sometimes told: 'It's too big.' I suppose I think about theatre performance much more and film is a secondary matter to me.

What was your most challenging role to date?
I would have to say Madame Ranyevskaya in Chekhov's *The Cherry Orchard* (1999). It is one of the great roles for a woman and I came to it very nervously. I was intimidated by the history of the role and knew that I was generally seen to be a funny character lady and not a tragic figure. I knew that there would be people who would think it impertinent of me to tackle the role and I was aware of a certain defiance in me that was not helpful in the development of the character. By the end of a difficult rehearsal process, I felt that I had created a credible figure and the production was met with critical approval. Much of Ranyevskaya is about the contrast of interior and exterior; inside, she is a melancholy woman, but she plays at being the young girl and the romantic. The part requires subtlety and suggestiveness, light emotional tints which point towards a more troubled, hidden self. That was difficult to achieve since I had often played characters who wear their hearts on their sleeves.

Do you find criticism helpful?
Actors tell the truth in performance but not backstage, and perhaps this is right – you know if your performance has been good or bad. I don't read reviews until six months after I've played the part because when I'm performing I can find a bad review crushing. Similarly, I read reviews of other performances after I've seen the production in question; criticism can colour one's view in a way that is unhelpful.

What do you think are your strengths?

I like big parts. I'm a character actress who has a high opinion of herself (not always shared by others!). I like dark, tough and unyielding parts, which I think surprises many people because of course I am predominantly known as a comic actress. I don't want theatre to be a comfort to people and I want to be cast in dramas like Eugene O'Neill's *Long Day's Journey into Night*, and am drawn to the bleakness of contemporary plays like Martin McDonagh's *The Beauty Queen of Leenane*. Comedy has come easily to me but I would rather make people cry. Comedy is about appearance and physicality and it's about instinct and timing; of course there's a lot to be learned but you can also be born with the gift. I'm very nervous before I go on stage but larger than life once I start performing.

I think I will be remembered most for my own show *Dickens's Women*, and I do feel that it is important work. To convey the work of Dickens to others, to try and instil my passion for this author in others, are real challenges. It's my interpretation of Dickens's England, my view of the class system. Dickens's world of excess meshes well with my own excess, and I think I can say without any modesty whatever that my Mrs Gamp is the best Mrs Gamp that has ever hit the stage. In that specific performance I can say that I transcended myself and that I achieved moments of great acting. All actors have to be realistic about commercial realities, and parts as leading lady have not been offered many times in my life because of my looks; consequently, I will reach a point which is near the top of my profession but will not reach the very top. With *Dickens's Women*, I know that I have performed to my full potential and at points that I matched the best actors, and I therefore know that it's possible to attain the same heights on other work in the future.

Linda Marlowe

Linda Marlowe, an actor and director, was born in Sydney, Australia and came to live in England at the age of ten. Her acting credits include *Decadence* (1981–7), *The Trial* (1973), *Metamorphosis* (1986), *Hamlet* (1979–83), *Greek* (1981) and *Coriolanus* (1997) – all directed by Steven Berkoff. She has been directed by Richard Jones in *Too Clever By Half* (1988) and *A Flea in her Ear* (1989), and has acted with the Royal Shakespeare Company in *The Virtuoso* (1991–2) and *The Theban Trilogy* (1991–2). Her television credits include *Floodtide*, *The Avengers*, *The Ruth Rendell Mysteries*, *Lovejoy*, *The Green Man*, Lynda La Plante's *She's Out*, *Silent Witness* and *Dalziel and Pascoe*; film work includes *Big Zapper*, *Becket*, *The Man Outside*, *Mr Love*, *Manifesto* and *The House of Mirth*. She has directed many plays, including *Lunch* by Steven Berkoff, Franz Xavier Kroetz's *Through the Leaves* and Arthur Miller's *A View from the Bridge*. In 2000–01 she appeared in a one-woman show, *Berkoff's Women*, compiled from the works of Steven Berkoff and directed by Josie Lawrence.

What was your training?
I started out intending to be a ballerina and went to ballet school, but abandoned dance and went to the Central School of Speech and Drama when I was seventeen. I was very young and, in some ways, if I'd ever listened to my teachers I would never have become an actress. Drama school took away my confidence and I was repeatedly told that I had a speech impediment. After I'd left, I saw Laurence Olivier's voice teacher, Iris Warren, who told me that I had no significant impediment, that I certainly had a slight lisp but also an unusually deep and attractive voice that I should use to my advantage.

The Central School philosophy of acting focused a great deal on the psychology of playing a character, but I learned most through doing, not talking, and my real training was provided by my subsequent work in repertory theatre in the 1960s. I feel strongly that an actor must develop their own tool-kit of skills because directors cannot always be relied upon; in the beginning, I worked with poor and even destructive directors, and I rapidly learned how to combat their lack of professionalism. If a director isn't helpful in rehearsal, then actors must be able to work on their own at home.

How did you break into professional work?
While I was at drama school, I was lucky enough to be cast as a karate-chopping heroine in a film called *Big Zapper* which did well, and I acquired an influential agent who believed in me and wanted to promote me for big movies. I was much more drawn towards theatre and didn't want to be pushed into film before I'd learned my craft, so I changed agent and began working in weekly repertory theatre. The regime required extraordinary discipline: we started a play on Monday, reading it through in the morning and beginning the blocking in the afternoon; from Tuesday to Thursday we did rehearsals in the morning and learned our lines in the afternoon; and on Fridays and Saturdays we did full run-throughs of the play without the book. The process began again on Monday with a different play, and you have to remember that we were performing in the evenings. The speed of the process was terrifying but it was the best possible training for theatre. There wasn't time to psychologize and develop character a great deal and I worked on my instincts; today, I'd find the process dissatisfying because I'd be aware of how much further I could explore a character. Directors did little more than block the play at that time; they told us about the set and plotted out our moves and had a very functional role. Blocking is old-fashioned now and directors don't work like that any more.

My first experience of a more extended rehearsal time and a long run of a play was at the Gate Theatre in Dublin, which was run by Micheál MacLiammóir. I learned a huge amount from the other actors, especially from Eithne Dunne, who was a tremendous actress, liked a drink and had a habit of citing the wrong lines from the wrong scene, but who consequently kept me on my toes and forced me to be inventive about finding ways of getting back to the correct lines in the correct scene! The play was *Forests of the Night* (1964) and the director, Louis Lentin, gave me a very good foundation in the construction and development of character.

What draws you to theatre?
It's so rewarding. It's live and the audience almost becomes the other characters for me. They may not realize how they help you to soar and shine. In those moments when you can feel that people are on the edge

of their seats, I experience an extraordinary buzz, and the exultation that you feel when you know that you are transporting people is indescribable.

How do you work on character?
I love working through improvisation, so initially I put the script to one side and take an aspect of a character and work on it physically. Some directors work in this way and others don't, but I always need to work on physicality for myself. There are all sorts of exercises used in rehearsal. When I played Blanche Dubois, one of my favourite characters, in Tennessee Williams's *A Streetcar Named Desire*, the director used a particular exercise which I found very helpful: we had to try and divulge what each character wanted from the other and then deny it. The actor playing Stanley, Blanche's brother-in-law, was instructed not to give me a drink, and this began an interesting pattern of body language between us: he recoiled inwardly at my character and I recoiled physically at his.

I use whatever I can to get a sense of character. I work out how they sit, stand, how they walk, what sort of shoes they wear and whether they can look others in the eye or not. I find that an exaggerated repetitive gesture may help me to find their physicality; the gesture usually doesn't end up in the production but is a way of orienting myself. Before I get on to the text, I need the freedom to talk, improvise, and to see what spills out of me.

You worked with Steven Berkoff for many years. How was that?
Steven saw me in an experimental theatre piece at a fringe theatre in London, directed inspirationally by Howard Panter (who is now a very successful producer) and liked my work. I was searching for something beyond conventional theatre and Berkoff set up a meeting. I saw his production of *Agamemnon* in Manchester and thought his performance was staggering. I first worked with him on his adaptation of Kafka's *The Trial* (1973), which was a choral ensemble piece. I was completely in awe of him and new to the ensemble, which made it very hard. I found his criticism brutal and actually left the production. He pursued me determinedly, then he hired someone else for all of fifteen minutes before deciding they were disastrous and demanded that I return unless I wanted to ruin his show. I did go back, but once the show was finished I made a decision not to work with him for a while because I was still too

scared. Without professional pressures, our friendship had time to flourish. In the meantime, I'd formed a punkish rock band with three other women, called the *Sadista Sisters*, and we landed a record contract and toured Europe for three and a half years. I put a lot of Berkoff's ideas into the presentation and spectacle of *Sadista Sisters*, and came to admire his passion and management through touring. I learned so much from playing to all kinds of audiences: at the Reading Festival we played to 30,000 and elsewhere there were small groups packed into cellars or bars. From 1979, I worked with Berkoff intensively over about a decade and our working relationship soared: I had matured, got the measure of him, knew how to fend for myself, and enjoyed the work.

Can you describe Berkoff's work?
Steven attended the Ecole Jacques Lecoq, but wanted to adapt mime to illustrate the spoken word. His project has been about the creation of his own brand of mime in combination with text, often his own plays and adaptations. He wanted to get away from elaborate, large sets and props or 'toys' as he called them, and persuade audiences of the reality of mime. I learned from watching and imitating him at work. I stood alongside and copied him, rather in the manner of copying a ballet master, and I think my dance training helped because I was not put off if he criticized me – dancers have to get a movement right and precision is critical to Steven. I watched how he created pictures with his body and how he held his hands. He created a physical body language and made us work with tableaux a great deal. Steven has even shown me how to play women; Mrs Grubach in *The Trial* was an extraordinary caricature of a woman, something I could never have arrived at without his suggestions.

When I did *Metamorphosis* (1987), Steven directed me to move in a very stylized way, like a marionette. Steven doesn't work on or discuss 'character' in rehearsals but is more interested in aesthetic formalism, so at home I worked on Mrs Samsa's character in the way I have described; I found her manner of sitting, walking and standing, worked out how she would erupt at her husband, and explored the pity, horror and disgust she felt for her son, Gregor. As an actor, I wanted to find something beneath the stylization; if I do not *feel* like someone else, my motivation for the performance is affected. Steven was delighted with the result and remarked that I'd brought a full-bodied character to Mrs Samsa and given her many dimensions.

How did you work on text with Berkoff?

Steven has a passion for poetry and rhetorically complex prose – the writers he returns to again and again are Kafka, Shakespeare and Poe. He always stresses the physical act of articulation and demands that actors give every word its full value, just as a musician has to strike every note. He always told actors not to rush their words and also encouraged us to play with them, stretch them, pop them and treat them as though they were physical entities. Steven was often more interested in the musicality of the voice, the soaring quality of delivery, the sounds of words than he was in meaning. He can be radically experimental; he often fragmented speeches, but I always wanted to keep a thread of meaning and made sure that I did not break the rhythm of a speech too many times. Berkoff's own writing is very hard to perform and there can be huge speeches and swathes of non-naturalistic dialogue, but I've developed techniques of handling it and I still go through it analytically, asking myself what my character is saying and what their intent is. I love Steven's writing; in my one-woman show, I've adapted a short story that he wrote about a lonely woman. His turns of phrase are extraordinary and he has a huge faculty for imagery; some audience members have been so struck by the piece that they think I must be relating events from my own life.

What was your experience in the Royal Shakespeare Company?

I think the RSC is in danger of becoming bland. I played Jocasta in *Oedipus Rex* (1991–2) and was Lady Gimcrack in Thomas Shadwell's *The Virtuoso* (1991–2); I enjoyed the experience to a degree but don't think that there is a commitment to developing actors or cherishing them. There are fewer parts for women than there are for men in the RSC and this has always been the case, and very often the roles that are counted as 'big', like Gertrude in *Hamlet*, are very important in terms of the play but do not mean very much in terms of the time you spend on stage.

I worked with director Nancy Duiguid in Howard Brenton's *Sore Throats* (1988) and found her strategies for improvisation enlightening. The play is about an abused wife who sinks to the depths of misery but decides to change her life. For one of the improvisations, Nancy gave me a bottle of wine and instructed me not to say anything for an hour: it was an interesting exercise and gruelling because I went through a threshold of boredom, emptiness and tiredness and began to feel isolated and locked inside myself. It gave me an insight into the emotional life of the character, and I found that her exercises made me question all sorts of things about the play and the character and forced me to plunge the depths of the writing. Nancy also used certain Stanislavskian exercises which I found less helpful. I had to identify an action in every line, such as: I weep, I demand, I renounce, I resent. I thought that it took away from the spontaneity and found it inhibiting, but I could see that for actors starting out, or for actors who need stringent directions, it could be useful. On the whole, it was very good to work with a woman director, because when I first started acting there simply weren't any women in that role other than Joan Littlewood in London.

Do you think that there is a lack of large parts for women in general?
Yes, it's a problem. The reason I'm now doing a one-woman show is because I wanted to explore and show the range and maturity of my acting. I wanted a real challenge, so I decided to create my own opportunity. I recently turned down a part in a stage adaptation of Patricia Highsmith's novel *Strangers on a Train*; it was another critical female role amounting to relatively few lines and I neither want nor need to do it. I want to be in the West End as a *tour de force* in my own right. I don't want to use up my talent on minor roles.

What was it like working with Richard Jones?
Richard had seen my work for Berkoff. He's a big opera director and has done massive projects like *The Ring* at Covent Garden and the Broadway musical *Titanic*. Richard's conception of theatre and opera is based on visual experimentation and he works with designers for weeks. I played a character called Auntie Cleopatra in Rodney Ackland's version of *Too Clever By Half* (1988). Cleopatra is an ageing woman who falls in love with a man who only wants to exploit her, a fact she discovers when she is dumped. The play and part are quite conventional, but Richard's direction turned the show into an extraordinary visual phantasmagoria. Three months before rehearsals, Richard told me that he had an idea that I should use prosthetics for the part and asked whether I had any ideas about Cleopatra's physicality. There is a moment when Cleopatra is referred to as possessing 'the face of a horse' and I decided that perhaps I should play the part with large false teeth. Richard sent me to a Harley Street dentist who built me the teeth. I had to teach myself to speak clearly when I was wearing them and at first could barely speak at

all, and I also found that I developed certain mannerisms for the character because of the teeth; for example, I developed a loud laugh during which I also caught my breath. The costumes by Richard Hudson were also fantastical: I began the show in a pink dress, a black wig and pointe shoes. In a conventional production, my part would not have been nearly so inventive, but Richard's directorial vision created a character who was both outrageous and moving. His instructions to actors were short-cut ways of obtaining unusual results: there's a scene in which Cleopatra is simply talking to another woman, but Richard told us to imagine that we were both in a powder-room; as a result, I was putting on make-up throughout the scene, which made it quirky and full of zest.

How has your directing informed your acting?
I was reluctant at first, and began by directing Berkoff's *Lunch* in 1983 at the Library Theatre in Manchester. Paul Kerryson encouraged me to direct full-length plays and I went on to Miller's *A View from the Bridge* (1990) and Martin Sherman's *A Madhouse in Goa* (1990), for which I won the *Manchester Evening News* Award for Best Director. Since then, I have directed quite a bit. I am not a conceptual director who has grand visions, but I do know what actors go through in rehearsal and can see things from their point of view. I understand their technical problems and can help them to find ways of overcoming them. Steven Berkoff always said that actors should direct and thinks it's vital that actors pass on their experience and skills to others, and I found that I could teach about physicality and mime. Actors can potentially make wonderful directors because they know how to create environments in which actors feel comfortable and they know how to deal with an actor's block. I know that what I want as an actor is a licence to experiment and not to feel self-conscious. Many directors make actors feel foolish, whereas they should feel that they could dare to do anything. On the other hand, directors can feel lonely during rehearsals, especially if things are going badly. I think I can be patient as a director because I am also an actor. I see acting and directing from both sides, but both are equally frightening.

Do you find acting for film different from acting for theatre?
I think in film there is a much greater probability that one will be typecast. The film and television industries are more fixated with appearance than theatre. Process does not differ greatly because actors have to

find truth and reality whatever the medium. In film and television, there isn't the same opportunity to rehearse but the work at home is the same as it would be for theatre. Of course, the acting style is usually smaller for the camera, especially in the case of close-ups, and you act more internally and a good deal more with the eyes. But there are moments when you have to act in a larger way for film too: I was recently filming for *Midsomer Murders* and had to rush up to a woman and attack her frenziedly; many on the set wondered at my energy, but I think that many people in film lack a bravery which comes from the danger of performing live in theatres – the theatre actor develops a courage and pluck which comes with the territory. I think it's much harder to move from film to theatre than vice versa. For theatre you need a whole set of technical accoutrements connected with developing the voice and keeping the body trim; you have to be able to project your voice and move fluidly; whereas in film you can get away with less. Television and film are money-earners for me and supplement my theatre income.

How did you develop your one-woman show, Berkoff's Women?
I was frustrated with limited acting roles and Steven encouraged me to take the power into my own hands. It was his idea that I do a show built on his material. I gave myself the opportunity to show as many different aspects of my skills as possible, so I play victims, tyrants and raucous and outrageous women. I play in naturalist and non-naturalist styles, and I bring a lot of myself to the show too. I would say, as Miriam Margolyes says of her Dickens show, that I am now consistently achieving my best work.

Conrad Nelson

Conrad Nelson was born and brought up in Liverpool. An actor, director and musician, he trained at Leicester Polytechnic. He has enjoyed a very diverse acting career and has worked extensively for Northern Broadsides theatre company and in plays by the poet Tony Harrison. His theatre acting credits include, for Northern Broadsides, *Antony and Cleopatra* (1996–7), *Romeo and Juliet* (1996), *Dracula* (1997), *The Mysteries* (1997), *Richard III* (1998), *Twelfth Night* (1999), *Much Ado About Nothing* (2000), *Alcestis* (2000) by Ted Hughes, *King John* and *The Merry Wives of Windsor* (both 2001); for Harrison, *The Trackers of Oxyrhynchus* (1989), *Poetry or Bust* (1993), *The Kaisers of Carnumtum* (1995) and *The Labourers of Herakles* (1995). His film credits include Kenneth Branagh's *Much Ado About Nothing*, Mike Ockrent's *Dancin' Thru' the Dark* and Joy Whitby's *Arion and the Dolphin*. His television work has included roles in *Casualty*, *The Bill*, *Coronation Street*, *Over the Rainbow* and *The Piglet Files*.

What was your training?
I started out by doing a three-year degree in Performing Arts at Leicester Polytechnic. I had no idea about drama schools and I'd attended Wirral Grammar School where the expectation was to go on to university rather than an acting school. The degree at Leicester gave me a foundation in acting, dance, music and arts administration; you could choose what you wanted to specialize in, but each of the disciplines was validated and seen to overlap with the others, so the ethos was very positive. Over the years, I've talked to many actors about their experiences at drama school and have found that one narrative predominates: the sense that they were brutally taken apart and then rebuilt, as though certain things had to be knocked out of them before they would make acceptable actors. The ethos at Leicester was just the reverse: every skill you had was utilized.

Do you think there is a significant difference between film and theatre acting?
Within the theatre environment alone there is a tremendous range of possible experiences. Live performance varies, an epic play in a Greek

amphitheatre is very different from a naturalist play in a small studio. Acting experience in film varies too, but the whole process of film is exciting in a different way: you're surrounded by cameras, the set, lights and the crew – so the sheer activity around you is energizing. Obviously in live performance the audience is generating energy, and in theatre you have the chance to refine a role night after night. Film does not allow the actor the luxury of that refinement.

You've worked extensively with the poet Tony Harrison. Could you talk about your experience?
I began by appearing in Harrison's play *The Trackers of Oxyrhynchus* at the Royal National Theatre in 1989. I was playing one of the trackers and had never acted at the National before. In retrospect, I realize that I landed the part because I was not afraid of the physicality that the play demands, nor was I alienated by the rhythm of the language. The rehearsals were very structured and concentrated on choric speaking and movement; the rhythm of the words set the physical confines of the play and I felt at ease with their music. Seven years later, *Trackers* was staged again at the West Yorkshire Playhouse and I played the role of Apollo – it was very satisfying as an actor to have made the journey from chorus to protagonist in the same play. The role was tremendously challenging – while I played Apollo, I also played the figure of an archaeologist, Granville, who becomes possessed by Apollo. During rehearsals I had to create two people and find not just a psychological understanding but also different vocal and physical languages for both. At some points I was speaking with the voice of Apollo but doing the actions of Granville being possessed by Apollo. I did a great deal of work on my own to find the physical languages and I prioritized the telling of the story by thinking about the visual pictures that I wanted to convey with my body. Then I presented my ideas to the rest of the actors and the director and they were able to help me sort out what did and didn't work. If they didn't understand what I was trying to convey, I refined the body work until they did; of course, the director was also selecting what worked and what did not. It's vital as an actor to be constantly asking yourself what the audience will perceive and what they will understand from your performance.

For *Poetry or Bust*, which Harrison wrote specifically for performance in a former wool-combing shed called Salts Mill in Yorkshire, I acted and composed the music. Then I acted in two epic plays: *The Kaisers of*

Carnuntum (1995), performed in a Roman amphitheatre in Austria, and *The Labourers of Herakles* (1995), which we played on an excavated site on the side of a mountain in Greece. These last two plays were spectacular one-off pieces of theatre and my parts were written specifically for me – both were quite extraordinary and unique theatrical experiences. Most of the time in theatre, you are delivering lines to an audience who are reasonably close, but the scale of an amphitheatre is overwhelming: you stand centre stage and deliver your lines out front and, though there are elements of realism, your style cannot be naturalistic. The scale of *Kaisers* was mind-blowing because the cast was composed of hundreds and hundreds of people: there were huge choirs, assemblies of horn-players and cellists, real lions and real tigers. I was pushed onstage by a brown bear and began by singing in a falsetto voice. We attempted a dress rehearsal but there was a storm, so the first night was the first attempt at a run-through. It was like organizing an army. On the second night a bear escaped and ran through the auditorium and took half an hour to round up. The adrenalin rush was phenomenal!

Given your interest in music and song, are you particularly conscious of developing your voice?
The body and voice are the only tools an actor has. I used to find physical theatre more interesting than Stanislavsky, though now I enjoy both challenges. Twenty-four hours of improvisation in a space appealed to me more than discussion of a text, and Stanislavsky's psychological approach to character is just one route available to an actor and not the only route. Over the years, I have attended dozens of workshops concentrating on different aspects of performance and generally I have learned from them all.

The correct use of the voice is vitally important and once a performer is in a large space, there's an instinct to shout and strain the voice. When I was at Leicester, I read about Roy Hart's voice techniques and became absolutely fascinated by him and his theories. Hart worked on the development of an eight-octave voice, a huge vocal range, through following a particular regime of exercises. He wanted the voice to achieve its ultimate range and argued that as we grow up, various restraints are exerted on us which reduce the power of the voice; a child's scream, for example, can be incredibly powerful but we rarely reach for that pitch again beyond a certain age. I was very keen on his work and visited him in his studio in the south of France. He's dead now, but there's still a school which promotes his practice.

I acted in Kenneth McLeish's *Omma* (1995), which was a complex acting challenge because it is scored: I was speaking to time, telling a story with music playing in the background, and you cannot mistime, otherwise you spoil the effect, but I enjoyed the exquisite precision that was required of me. It was like performing to an unstoppable, elaborate musical metronome.

How did you become involved with Northern Broadsides?
I met Barrie Rutter, the Artistic Director of Northern Broadsides, when I was doing *Trackers* at the National. He led a mask workshop and I liked the muscularity and dynamism of the acting and the directness of the audience address. Barrie wanted to reclaim northern accents and perform classic texts with regional voices; he wanted actors to be who they are, to carry their origins on to the stage with them instead of being required to speak received (southern) English. So he works with actors from the north and is dedicated first and foremost to audiences in the north. It was actually the freshness and accessibility of the acting style that drew me to the company – not the strength of feeling I have about my slight Liverpool accent. The company have worked on Greek classical texts, Shakespeare, Harrison, and premièred Ted Hughes's *Alcestis* (2000). The repertoire requires a lot of verse speaking, but the physical dimensions of the acting are interesting; one of the most memorable scenes I've done is from *Richard III* (1992), in which the battle was choreographed as a clog dance and the sound of our stamping feet thundered around the auditorium.

Actors at Northern Broadsides are very experimental in terms of where they perform. I don't always bless them because I've been in some grim situations. Audience members have passed out from the cold in Saltaire, Yorkshire, and I've rarely been as freezing as the time we performed at Shipton cattle market. The unhealthiest and dankest venue was a viaduct. In Brazil, one of the sites was so vast, it was impossible to know how to focus yourself and the acoustics were difficult to fathom. On the other hand, it's given me a set of unique experiences: performing *The Merry Wives of Windsor* (1993) in plastic raincoats in driving rain was not especially uplifting, but the audience simply put up their umbrellas and were quite unperturbed. When we performed *Richard III* at the Tower of London, the atmosphere was electric; in the very first scene, Clarence is under armed guard and actually being escorted to the Tower: it set the whole play alight and the tension was incredible. I remember a scene when it started to rain as Richmond and Richard began to fight, and on the line 'The bloody dog is dead', the rain stopped. The open air can outstrip the most technologically advanced production.

Do you find realist styles less challenging?
Categorizing a performance in a rigid way is not a useful exercise and it too often oversimplifies the complexities of a production. I don't understand actors who have contempt for naturalist styles. I've just done a workshop with Mike Alfreds: it was driven by Stanislavskian principles but the exercises had been adapted. We worked on improvising dialogue, played characters' intentions and concentrated on stagecraft. Mike asked us to look at the performing area and find the best place to stand and tell a story. He asked us to identify the coldest spot and then the hottest spot. He asked us to think about what an actor looks like crossing from stage left to stage right and vice versa. What is the effect from entering stage left, or stage right? What is the effect of walking upstage to downstage? I thought about aspects of stagecraft that I'd never considered before and found it enlightening and valid. It's important to work with actors and directors who have completely different approaches: it forces you to try out new things. Actors need to think about the management of their director. I have to find the best route to get the best work out of myself and out of the director. I like to have a large input into my roles, which affects the decisions I make about who I want to work with, but at the same time I can't act in a bubble and I have to be responsive to those around me.

Have you been strongly influenced by any particular actors?
No, there are no icons. I watch actors intently and I absorb, steal and test out whatever strikes me as interesting. I find Richard Briers's facility to touch his audiences impressive, and I admire Kenneth Branagh's drive and ability; it was extraordinary in the film of *Much Ado About Nothing* to watch him play Benedick and then hear him call his own cut as he left the frame.

What's your experience of performing with a mask?
One of the first exercises the performer does is pick up the mask, look at it and try to work out what the features are expressing. The performer

then seeks to physicalize the mask through their body. This may sound simple but the precision required is absolute: the performer's toe need only be slightly stiff or their knee bent at the wrong angle and the endeavour to create a specific image becomes meaningless. Physically, it's as though the body is under a microscope and every movement, every position is under critical scrutiny. Once the back of the head is seen, the illusion is broken, so the performer learns not to turn their head too much. Recently I tried out some of the masks used by Trestle Theatre Company and it was fascinating to explore the physical worlds that opened up just by placing them over my head. Some actors feel as though they undergo a change of identity when they wear a mask, they feel they have been transported elsewhere, but I try to concentrate on what I am communicating and not on what I may be feeling.

Wearing a mask is a disorientating experience: the performer may believe that they are conveying a very specific picture but in fact they may be portraying something completely different. Even the so-called neutral mask has its own life and requires precision. The discipline is to listen to the other actors and to be able to take your cue from what they are saying. With time, I've found that I've gained a physical vocabulary and have much more of a sense about how I need to move in order to give a particular effect. I've learned to adjust my vocal and physical registers through playing in so many different kinds of venue.

How did your career as a composer for theatre begin?
I studied acting at college but always had a keen interest in music, and I volunteered to write music for Northern Broadside's *The Merry Wives of Windsor*. I began writing basic tunes and have since branched out. I write from the point of view of being part of the production and make the music an integral element of the production, not an awkward moment that jars. At first I was quite defensive, but now I'm more prepared to share my ideas and voice doubts. I have a lot of big ideas in my head which I'd like to develop in the future, but there's still a great deal I have to learn first – much of the enjoyment lies in learning.

Do you pay heed to critics?
Actors have to remind themselves that a critic is only representative of his or her own voice. Sometimes a critic's interpretation is very constructive, in the sense that it contextualizes the production in a new way or throws an interesting light on a particular aspect of the performance.

Sometimes when I've had doubts as an actor but it has not been useful to voice them to the director, I've found it comforting that a critic has reinforced my private view. If actors read reviews of their work, they must be prepared to take the knocks. Every theatre-goer is a critic of sorts, but the reality is that a journalist's view can affect future audiences, especially in London, and Northern Broadsides, for example, finds the aloofness of London audiences quite problematic. A caustic comment can begin a process of anxious self-examination which can disrupt an actor's confidence.

How do you see yourself developing?
I want to keep acting, composing and directing: for me, they all overlap and feed into each other. I'd like to take on more parts in new plays; I love the classical repertoire but I'm always conscious of the heritage of the part I'm playing and would like to play roles which I feel I could create from new. Barrie Rutter is encouraging me to direct for Northern Broadsides and I'm excited by that prospect: I know who I want to work with and I can be confident in the experience I have amassed. All the administrative frameworks are in place, so it is a golden opportunity to focus solely on the artistic side.

Ruth Posner

Ruth Posner was born in Poland and escaped from the Warsaw ghetto as a child in 1938. She trained with London Contemporary Dance, took a Masters Degree in Theater Arts at New York University and did courses at the Uta Hagen Drama Studio in New York. Her theatre work includes *The Dybbuk* (Royal Shakespeare Company, 1995), *Blood Wedding* (1997), *Theresa* (1990–2000), *The Holocaust Trilogy* (1990–2000) and the *Millennium Dome Show* (2000). Her film and television work includes *Leon the Pig Farmer*, *Bramwell*, *Making News*, *Casualty*, *Sin Bin*, *Love Hurts* and *The Ruth Rendell Mysteries*.

You always wanted to be an actress but came to it late. Why was that?
It's complicated and the reasons were part psychology and part force of circumstance. My Aunt Lola and I were the only members of the family to escape from the Warsaw ghetto and the reason that I survived was that my father had organized forged identity papers for me. I was only ten, but my 'acting' career could be said to have begun then. My parents died in extermination camps and so did all other family members. I came to England and was housed in a hostel for refugees; I wanted to be an actress as a teenager, but after my experience in Poland I was rather ashamed of the ambition because it seemed frivolous. I was encouraged to qualify in something which would later support me, which made good sense given my situation, so I did a three-year teacher-training course at the London College of Dance and Drama. The courses were general ballet, tap, folk dance and Isadora Duncan-inspired movement classes. How I got in I will never know. I was the only Jew and the only foreigner, but I was treated like a mascot and, actually, because no one could place me, I avoided the tortures of the English class system!

I wasn't stimulated by the courses and, to cut a long story short, I married at eighteen and went to Israel. There I met a dancer from the States who had been trained by Martha Graham; I'd never seen anything like it, the style had such depth and theatricality. I spent four years training and performing on a kibbutz. When I returned to England, dance was divided between ballet and musicals and there was nothing contemporary. I met Robin Howard, also a Martha Graham devotee, who founded London Contemporary Dance in 1968, and worked there for twelve years. Though Martha Graham's style is now established, our work back then provoked powerful criticism, not least because the style is sexual (though not sexy) and many were outraged by it. My entry into theatre came when I began teaching movement classes at the Royal Academy of Dramatic Art. I was an inventive and successful teacher and worked on pieces like Beckett's short plays. It was difficult for me to find work as an actress; I had an accent in the days when only Received Pronunciation was acceptable and only a few directors would take the 'risk' of giving me work. When my husband and I moved to New York in the 1970s, I turned more fully to acting and undertook specific training. But the lateness with which I came to acting is connected both with my fear of failure (that's why I kept running away from it) and my husband's lack of encouragement. I'm not blaming him; he simply couldn't understand why I wanted to act and perhaps he was threatened by the idea. Now that I'm an old woman, he doesn't have any qualms!

What was your experience of actor training in New York?
Drama studios proliferated in 1970s New York, and most of them were Method oriented. Uta Hagen had written an influential book, *In Respect of Acting*, which was influenced by Strasberg's Method but was not quite so messianic. The stress was on observation, accuracy and the search for what was called 'truth'. I thought what was generally lacking was adequate work on the physical and the vocal; the approach was very analytical and psychological, but actors were not taught how to project their voices or how to move fluidly. I think it still holds true today to say that the emphasis on detailed naturalistic work means that American actors are usually very good on film but less well prepared for theatre work, especially Restoration or Shakespearean performance.

You also went to Japan to train with Tadashi Suzuki and performed in a Japanese Noh play in London. What drew you to Japanese performance?
I saw a Japanese company perform *The Trojan Women* in London in 1986 and was knocked out by the whole experience. It was a synthesis of text, sound, movement and image, and each element was performed to perfection. I wrote to Suzuki's school and asked whether I could train with him, but was told that I was too old. I persisted and explained that I was a trained dancer and that I was disciplined about physical exercise and was finally permitted to attend. Suzuki's methods are now widely

used on drama courses in the States, though I think they are generally misunderstood and misapplied.

I found Suzuki's exercises illuminating and they provided me with a real awakening as a performer; it's about finding core physical energy and total mental concentration, and the physical routines he has devised are very demanding. Suzuki also has specific ways of doing choral work, developed from Kabuki, Noh and Tae Kwondo, and is able to create an extraordinarily powerful effect. I found my voice technique improved so much that I could speak an octave lower. I think Suzuki's methods are essentially about the creation of a powerful performance presence, and I quote Peter Brook's sentence from *The Empty Space* whenever I am asked to sum up Suzuki's investigations: 'An actor is a body in space and being still is the result of the body that can move, and not the limitation of the body that can't do any better.'

I then auditioned for a Noh play called *Komachi* in London and got the part. The play is about a woman who is dying but who must resolve everything in her life and wanders through the world, looking for peace. The only way for her to resolve the turmoil she feels about her ex-lover is to allow his body to enter hers, temporarily become the warrior he was and make her peace with him. I couldn't have done the performance without Suzuki's training. The director was Japanese and gave the most detailed but tiny notes, telling me to move my chin a fraction upwards, or extend my arm slightly. The precision is beyond anything that is found in Western theatre. I also used some of Suzuki's movement techniques when I acted the Old Moon in Lorca's *Blood Wedding*; I made a slow movement across stage while seeming not to move.

What motivated you to act?
I wanted to escape from myself and live vicariously through others. The older you get, the more you realize that there is no escape from yourself. I love rehearsing; the constant use of the imagination and the journey of discovery are thrilling to me. I can't think of anything else in life that gets a group of people working together to such a pitch of intensity. It creates a real sense of unity, though of course afterwards there's a let down because there is no continuity.

You worked on The Dybbuk *at the Royal Shakespeare Company. What was that like?*
I was offered a year's contract at the RSC when I was abroad acting in

Julia Pascal's *Dybbuk*. I went because I wanted to immerse myself in the experience of working with a large company. The director was Katie Mitchell and I thought the degree to which she researched a text was quite extraordinary. Her great strength is that she tries to re-create as far as possible the world of the play and I enjoyed every minute of rehearsal time. It was a six-week rehearsal process; for the first three weeks, we watched films, read piles of literature and tried to re-create that world in all sorts of ways. Many cast members didn't even know what a Hasidic Jew was, so Katie brought in Hasidic wigs and items from their everyday life for us to wear and touch. Katie made us draw, brought in an expert in Hasidic dance and tried in every way to bring that way of life alive for us. Not all the actors liked Katie's approach, but I had a fantastic time.

How do you prepare for playing a character?
Some directors tell you not to talk to them about your character and I go along with that. I read the script again and again. If you start out with a firm idea of character, you limit yourself with the end result. It's a difficult process because you're working in a vacuum, but I couldn't work with a director who wanted a clear idea of my character in the third rehearsal. I know that I discover things about my character through physical experimentation, and that's why I find radio such an incredible discipline; I have to cut my body out and put everything into my voice. Otherwise, I ask myself how the character might walk, or sit, or comb her hair, eat an apple or read a book. Sometimes I use the Method technique of 'actioning', where you ask of your character: why am I saying this? and try to answer with a verb: I command you, or I envy you, or I offend you. When a script demands a lot of interaction I find that this exercise helps because it teaches you to listen and react rather than just say the lines. Acting is *hard*; you don't simply speak, you have to concentrate and remain alive to every moment.

When I work with writer and director Julia Pascal, Method techniques are of no use whatever. Julia is influenced more by Central European non-naturalistic traditions and I'll often be playing several roles, so I have to swap between roles and totally change 'character'. It's almost like a circus technique, and you have to be able to change your physical presence and alter your vocal pitch; it's no use analysing the 'truth' in this sort of process, you simply need certain skills to be able to do it.

You've worked with Julia Pascal for many years. Could you talk about that?
Yes, I've acted in her plays *Theresa*, *The Holocaust Trilogy* and *The Yiddish Queen Lear*. I performed repeatedly in *Theresa* over a ten-year period. I'm indebted to Julia because acting in her plays has been so much more than a job, it's also been about political beliefs, challenging received history and not letting the Holocaust be forgotten. Theresa was based on Julia's research of a young woman who was sent to a concentration camp by the authorities on the island of Guernsey [part of the Channel Islands and part of Britain]. The Channel Islands were occupied during the Second World War and there was economic, administrative and in some cases political collaboration, and Jews were deported to camps if they were caught, while islanders who sheltered them risked their lives. *Theresa* shocked audiences in England, who were often unaware of the history of the Channel Islands, and it toured successfully on the continent.

Each time we came to perform *Theresa* during that ten-year period, we always changed it. From the first performance to the last, the play has altered totally. Julia lets the actors have a great deal of input; if you show her something you've worked on yourself and it's effective, she accepts it and incorporates it into the show. Julia always provided narrative structure and we worked by improvisation, and often segments of dialogue or certain images or physical actions emerged from that. I did weary of *Theresa*, though it was one of the best theatrical experiences of my life; but I only need to read about revisionist, Holocaust-denying historians like David Irving and I'd agree to do it again. I did not, thankfully, have a sense of living with the character of Theresa over that ten years, but obviously the subject matter is personally very meaningful to me and at least one of the scenes in the play came directly from my own experience. The first time I worked on the play, we did an improvisation and I totally collapsed because I'd never revisited the deep part of myself which was so traumatized by events in my childhood. It was a very frightening primal experience, involving a cathartic outpouring of images in my head from the ghetto itself, and I sobbed and sobbed. After that, I wondered whether I could return to the material, because I knew I could not afford to let it affect me in the same way; it took time, and we took a break from rehearsals, but I did disentangle myself from the material and rediscover a professional position, largely by working very technically and not allowing images to intrude.

Julia also incorporates different languages into her plays and that's liberating for me. Julia asked me to improvise something in Polish and I wasn't sure that I could, but the experience was extraordinary – I felt such an emotional intensity. I've read Eva Hoffmann's work, *Lost in Translation*, and she talks about the mother tongue being a visceral part of us and secondary languages as operating more intellectually. Now actors are not required to lose their accents, but I really believe that when we are forced to speak in received ways, it can affect the personality.

Do you act differently for film?
Yes. I remember appearing in the television soap *Casualty*; I was required to become hysterical at a particular medical catastrophe. I acted it as I would in theatre and the director quietly took me to one side and said: 'All you have to do is think it!' I'd made a Greek tragedy out of it. I love the paraphernalia of filming, the crews and the sets, and I find the act of concentration a real challenge; cutting out all the activity around you is no small feat.

Do you have any acting ambitions?
I've never been interested in commercial success. The writer Bonnie Greer, who saw me perform in Julia's plays, says she wants to write something for me, which would be wonderful!

Hugh Quarshie

Hugh Quarshie was born in Ghana, West Africa, and moved to London between the ages of three and four. He grew up in north London and went to the University of Oxford, where he studied Politics, Philosophy and Economics. His acting career includes a stint for the Royal Shakespeare Company and time at the Schauspielhaus in Hamburg. His theatre credits include *Henry IV* (1983), *Romeo and Juliet* (1985–6), *The Rover* (1985), *Two Noble Kinsmen* (1985–6), *Macbeth* (1986) and *The Great White Hope* (1986), for which he won the *Plays and Players* Best Actor award. He was also nominated for the Laurence Olivier Award for his season at the Royal Shakespeare Company in 1985–6. In 1989, he appeared in *Ma Rainey's Black Bottom* at the Royal National Theatre. His film and television credits include *Star Wars: The Phantom Menace* and the highly acclaimed documentary drama *The Murder of Stephen Lawrence*.

What was your training?
I didn't go to drama school. I went to Oxford University and performed in the Drama Society, though little of what was done was original in terms of plays or the manner of their staging. Our work was imitative in the sense that we were really demonstrating how well we could emulate a West End style of acting. I learned all sorts of bad habits, which curiously were reinforced by later work in professional theatre, especially at the Royal Shakespeare Company.

What sort of bad habits?
I went on school trips to see the Royal Shakespeare Company and was struck even then by the fact that some individual performances were entirely theatrical and didn't point to a life outside theatre at all; they focused on theatricality and the conventions of acting rather than on non-theatrical reality. The actors had all been trained to speak in the same way and their voices had all been subject to the same company processing. I am suspicious of the workings of voice departments at our national theatres because they encourage the majority of actors to deliver their lines in a precious and unnatural way. Jonathan Miller once

described Margaret Thatcher's voice as being like a 'perfumed fart' and that phrase comes to mind when I hear the manufactured voices and see the accompanying styles of acting on mainstream stages! To my mind, England is still dominated by a legacy of florid acting from the past. Laurence Olivier's Othello seems laughable now, but at the time it was grand and came from a school of acting that looked like acting. I have admired actors like Bill Paterson and Tom Conti, who found a high level of naturalism in their verbal and physical delivery.

How did you become an actor?
By accident. I started out as a journalist and worked in a press-cuttings agency for radio and television broadcasting. After a year, I was going slightly crazy and left to do Theatre in Education (TIE) in the East End of London and in Nottingham. TIE was very much a 1970s phenomenon, and I left to join agit-prop theatre and acted for a black theatre company. Permitting no doubt about its politics, the show was called something like *Black Skins, White Chains* (1977–8) and it was schematic, didactic shit. I can only describe it as performance graffiti! It was so aggressively lowbrow that it catapulted me back into journalism, as a sub-editor. After that, I auditioned for *Whose Life is it Anyway?* (1979) and found myself in a show with Tom Conti. It was a turning-point for me, and I admired his skills. I acted in *Whose Life* for a year and feel now that I should also have persisted with my writing; at least you have control of the labour and you don't have to 'cook by committee' as you usually do when working with other actors and directors! Of all the people that I've acted with, two stand out: the late Colin Blakeley and Judi Dench. Both were technically so good and behaviourally so believable that they made me wonder whether I would ever be able to achieve their heights.

You've made it clear that you're disappointed with theatre in Britain. Why is that?
It's so easy to get locked into conventions and traditions. British theatre is still predominantly about white middle-class actors doing the plays of dead white males to white middle-class audiences. So many people both inside and outside the industry are disillusioned by its conservatism. Theatre becomes more and more like opera: it's expensive and élitist and most attempts to popularize it are heroic but fatuous: it's a minority pastime and cinema and television are the more democratic media, but

the price for that democracy is a continual dumbing-down. Writers and directors can exercise more control than actors, and acting is not financially attractive if you rely on theatre as a main source of income. The Royal Shakespeare Company demands a long commitment from an actor but pays relatively little: life is hard when you calculate for your mortgage and your extra rent and travel bills. There's also all the stress of martinet directors imposing their parochial views on you! The Royal Shakespeare Company used to cherish the idea of apprenticeship for actors, but these days only a few are singled out, groomed and invited back again. At the end of my first season, I received a postcard thanking me for my work and saying that there was no longer any work for me. There was no discussion of any further work and no attempt to develop my career. I found this event very upsetting and it was the first of many eye-openers for me. In an earlier era, there was much more pastoral care taken of actors at the RSC and a greater effort was made to further their career. It's very difficult for actors to earn a living and many turn to television, gain a profile and then return to the theatre, like John Nettles.

What about your early days?
When I started contemplating a career in theatre in the late 1970s and early 1980s, there weren't many distinguished black actors. The prevailing wisdom had been that black actors couldn't speak English with an indigenous accent and there was a belief that they tended to overact. There was a sense that writers and directors were waiting for a generation of black actors who could speak received English; I was part of that generation who was shouting 'Here we are!' and I thought that I had the advantage of a classical education. I joined the Royal Shakespeare Company in 1981 and my first part was Aaron the Moor in *Titus Andronicus* (1981). I felt that my talents were appreciated and I looked forward to a future there. I played Cleomenes in a dreary production of *The Winter's Tale* (1981), but my big break came when I was understudying for Tim Dalton and his contract expired before the end of the season. To my delight, and the amazement of many, I was offered Dalton's part, Hotspur in *Henry IV, Part I* (1983), which I played with relish and was critically well received. At the time, I had no idea that there was so much institutional hostility to my casting and I'm grateful to my colleagues for their good manners in only speaking of this behind my back. It was progress for black actors to shout the lines of dead white males, I suppose.

I think the most satisfaction I have gained through acting has been in modern plays: Howard Sackler's *The Great White Hope* (1985) was a fulfilling experience and so was August Wilson's *Ma Rainey's Black Bottom* (1989), and I enjoyed the challenge of Michael Bogdanov's and Howard Brenton's adaptation of Goethe's *Faust* (1995), also directed by Bogdanov. I look back on my nomination for an award for *Two Noble Kinsmen* (1985–6) with bemusement. The play has an interesting literary history and may raise questions as to its precise authorship, but it is not a good play structurally. The director did try to include me and the other actors in the creative evolution of the play, but I can't say that I understood the meaning or style of the play by the end of the process. I didn't know why we were doing the play, and I never quite believed in what we were doing.

You have said that you think the theatre industry promotes certain myths about black actors. What are those myths?

Black actors were traditionally associated with being strong physical presences, and their supposed animal passion was usually emphasized. I think of the films of the 1940s and 1950s and immediately see stereotypes of large female servants with rolling eyes, or glistening bodies of black slaves working in fields, or attendants carrying the litter holding the white queen or princess. Generally, black actors made it in musicals and were renowned for their singing and dancing. It's hard to think of many established black theatre actors in England who've come through a non-musical route: there are Adrian Lester and Josette Simon. The late Erroll John saw the lie of the land early on and left for the States. In a way, all of us are aspiring to please the tastes and absorb the ethos of the theatre establishment, which is itself based on a white, male, self-regarding exclusivity, and that's the terrible contradiction of our position. Michael Jackson's decision to whiten his skin is the extreme case of how far you can go to make yourself popular and acceptable. When I see footage of Jimi Hendrix at Woodstock, I'm struck by the fact that the number of black musicians on stage is greater than the number of blacks in the audience. In appealing to a prevailing ethos, there is a danger that blacks distance themselves more and more from their origins, and I am increasingly troubled by this dilemma. I speak English in a polished way and the irony is that speaking as well as I do disqualifies me from appearing in some of the grittier films.

There was a time when I used to say that the arts did the job that religion failed to do – remind us of our communality and spirituality, and offer us individual guidance from a creative spirit. We may lament the fact that the Archbishop of Canterbury has said that England is a nation of atheists, but perhaps it's a good thing that he said it and we can begin to reflect on and dissect this statement. I don't think we can any longer regard the classics as being a reflection of the society we live in and we need to interrogate them and find a different way of performing them.

It's assumed that Othello should be the part that every black actor wants to play. I beg to differ. Black actors have the same aspirations as other actors and want to play Hamlet! I'm very wary of playing Othello and have never accepted the role for theatre. I've explored the part on radio, but if I ever were to appear on stage as Othello, I could only do so having worked with a director who was prepared to question the text and adapt or change the speeches which are politically and performatively suspect. I think there's a real problem with the clumsiness of the dénouement and the recovery of Iago's self-incriminating letter to Roderigo, which is nonsensical as a device. I also find the construction of Othello's character problematic because it's based on the premise that once a black man's passion is aroused, he becomes homicidally jealous. The construction is founded upon racist literary conventions and theatrical conventions only serve to reinforce the suspect politics. Key passages need reinterpreting and there are lines in the play which I simply could not say because they equate black skin colour with moral impurity, lines that make it clear that the part was written for a white man with his face blacked up.

For a time I thought that I did have something to prove as an actor and that I should do my stint of the classics, but I'm not sure what I've proved at all and it gave me no artistic satisfaction. I've turned down parts that would have raised my profile significantly, but they were parts that I didn't feel reached the people with whom I wanted to communicate. I compare myself to a priest who has lost his faith. I used to think that the arts could remind audiences that there are many more things which unite individuals than divide them, but when I go to the theatre now, I feel no connection either with the actors on stage or with the people sitting next to me. The last time I felt excited was when I saw the Argentinian group De La Guarda at the Roundhouse in 1999. I am a member of a theatre-going class but I am not engaged by theatre and I don't think our common humanity is enhanced by it. We need to think about the democratic and social function of the arts.

Do you think the sterility you describe is a particular problem in England?
I worked at the Schauspielhaus in Hamburg when Michael Bogdanov was Artistic Director and had a thrilling and fascinating time there. I was initially aghast at the violence of actors' passions; at rehearsals they really laid into Michael and condemned the text a translation of *Guys and Dolls*. The audiences were equally as fervent. I played Tybalt in Michael's production of *Romeo and Juliet* and at the curtain call I received seventy per cent cheers and thirty per cent boos; it was extremely disconcerting, but the audience members wanted their voices heard. When Michael went out, the proportion of cheering and booing was reversed. Michael's tenure was always under fire from the German arts establishment and I thought he had incredible guts, but he just accepted their strength of feeling. He had been brought in on the promise of generating more productions; originally actors and directors had been allowed fifteen-week rehearsals and Michael cut the length of preparation down – though it was still a long time by English standards. I noticed that most German actors arrived at rehearsal having done their homework; they knew their lines and were pretty much word perfect; there was also always a prompter in rehearsal so you could put the book down and act from day one. The longer rehearsal time also gave you time to try out lots of things for yourself, show them to the director and see if they worked. You had time to test things out, change things, make mistakes. Six- to eight-week rehearsals are the ultimate luxury in England, and even then most English actors hold on to the book until the fifth week, so the director has real difficulty in knowing what he is getting from actors. I suppose the main difference is that in Germany actors commit early to decisions and in England actors commit themselves to decisions much later. Having said this, I was unusual: other black actors in Hamburg tended to be on rollerskates in *Starlight Express* or dressed in feline suits in *Cats*.

I admire German theatre and German actors: their performances are gritty, visceral and very powerful. The night I saw Peter Zadek's production of Wedekind's *Lulu*, about four people fainted during the murder scene. It was genuinely terrifying. Theatre *matters* to Germans, they take it seriously and they put a lot of financial resources in to it. I think theatre-going is more ritualistic in England; people go along in the same way that they go to church, but the experience is as solipsistic as riding the underground in the rush hour: everyone is pressed together but no one looks at anyone else and no one talks. It's a ritual that puzzles me and leaves me cold. I rather envy those people that flock to the West End and come away feeling fulfilled: it's not like that for me any more. I do think the work of the Royal Court should be championed, however, as should work at the Tricycle Theatre. There was a time in the late 1960s and early 1970s when theatre was exciting and there was a sense that it mattered more. I've wondered whether there's now more of a sense of a dialogue between audience and actor in regional theatres. I wish the flame of those theatre politics of thirty years ago was still burning, but there are only embers.

What do you make of the West End at the moment?
There have been a lot of American stars coming over, like Macaulay Culkin, Daryl Hannah and Kathleen Turner: you could see it as further evidence of internationalism, and certainly British actors have gone over to Broadway too; or you could see it as the impact of aggressive commercialism, of a belief that if you want to fill a theatre, you must have a star name. It's true to say that a narrow but rich vein of London audiences will pay a great deal to see a star appear in any old nonsense!

There are very few plays I've seen which I've found astonishing, and none of them were in the West End. My list would include Peter Brook's *Mahabarata*, Bogdanov's *Henry IV* and *Henry V*, Trevor Nunn's production of *Nicholas Nickleby* and Zadek's *Lulu*. I've performed a great deal, but there are only three productions which have satisfied me intellectually and artistically. Of course you have to mine a ton of rubble to find a gem, but when you spend your career mining and you only unearth rubble, it gets disheartening. My resolve has stiffened and I'm not prepared to be in anything where I feel the conventions don't mean anything. I'm in a dilemma and I'm not sure quite what to do: do I persevere or evolve my own style? A fantastic film role would allow me to retreat from theatre for a while and find my bearings again. I think there are obstacles for black actors in theatre: Britain has a heritage view of theatre based on a heritage view of Britain, which tends to bleach out black people in spite of documentary evidence showing that we've been living here for centuries. There's always been a refusal on the part of the British to accept that an element of their make-up is black. You see it in the reception of books like Emily Brontë's *Wuthering Heights*: it's clear that Heathcliff's dark looks imply that he is not wholly white, but it's all swept under the carpet and is explained away by his vague gypsy ancestry. I'm not sure whether the theatre establishment has opened its doors further or whether black actors have learned to find their way round the ethos and conventions of institutional obstacles.

The problems also go beyond colour and come back to the staleness of performance conventions in Britain. So many established actors are doing one-man or one-woman shows in the West End – Simon Callow, Miriam Margolyes, Ken Campbell, Patrick Stewart – and that must indicate that they do not feel challenged by the roles they are being offered or that they are unhappy with the restraints imposed on them by the way the system works. There is a world of difference between the word to be spoken and the word to be read, and the two are still far too blurred in English theatre. I enjoy language that fits in the mouth and isn't complete until it's spoken, but there is a literary influence in England that has held back more experimental styles of theatre. Michael Caine once said of the film industry: 'Americans make moving pictures and the English make talking pictures'; and Clint Eastwood joked about the film *Where Eagles Dare*, saying that 'Richard Burton does what he does best and speaks the lines beautifully; and I do what I do best: I shoot people.' The British have a reputation for their facility for speaking and acting from the neck upwards, and many actors are weary of that style, although Antony Sher is an actor who has really been trying to meld the vocal with the physical, and his performances as Richard III and Cyrano certainly fell into a bravura style of acting. I think the same could be said of my old colleague Gerard Murphy. It's time for a re-examination and reassessment of British theatre: restrained passion is clearly not the only path to be followed. I'm looking for and missing that sense that we are concerned with making closer contact with life outside theatre.

Have you experimented with different styles of acting?
I played Antony in Peter Hall's production of *Julius Caesar* (1995–6) and whilst I paid scrupulous regard to the structure of the play and to Hall's strict rules about verse-speaking, I also tried to find a greater informality in my acting. I took a critical hammering in the press, though the younger actors told me that they admired what I was doing, and I still think that audiences have an appetite for a style of acting that, to my mind, looks like acting.

Is there a difference between television and theatre acting?
If you've trained as a classical theatre actor, then you have to unlearn

your acting style for film. Many top theatre actors in England do not make the transfer into film and it's because of the way they were trained to speak. Ian McKellen, Patrick Stewart and Ben Kingsley have been able to move into film, but not by applying what they learned for stage. They have learned to speak more conversationally, though their style is still different from their American counterparts. Quite a few of the great names in acting left the Royal Shakespeare Company early to go into film; I'm thinking of Ralph Fiennes, but Peter O'Toole famously broke his contract to film *Lawrence of Arabia*. If you want a film career, it can be a powerful disadvantage to train as a classical theatre actor. The prevailing belief that a mastery of classical style enables you to act in any style is patently nonsense: there are different styles to be learned, just as there are different genres and performance conventions, and it is arrogant and stupid to claim that an actor's ultimate achievement must be playing the role of Hamlet or Othello.

What do you think of theatre criticism?
I think critics are lazy. Michael Bogdanov once did a survey of reviews for his production of *Faust*. He found an astonishing similarity of phrasing and commentary in the reviewing, which had come from the preface of the Penguin edition of the play and the publicity blurb. Critics concentrate on finding the *bon mot* and not the *mot juste*, and they rarely acknowledge that, like actors, they are also playing to an audience. It's irritating that they have the power to sway both actors and audiences, and I do not think that they are rising to the challenge of interrogating theatre at all. They are themselves a part of the establishment and can't see that it's a problem.

What are your ambitions?
At the moment I feel the dead weight of theatrical conventions and interpretations, and it's not that I think they should be thrown out wholesale, but I would like time to experiment. I wish that leading directors had the courage, the time and the money to rehearse and do a play in three months, as they used to in Germany. I think very interesting results would be yielded. Peter Brook has certainly demonstrated the value of taking time to explore texts with actors. I'm heartened that Adrian Lester is playing Hamlet and not Othello for Brook; it's very inspiring for me to see that black actors can be cast in such roles. I'd love to play the part of Falstaff, and I'd like the chance to explore the classics

in non-conventional ways. I would also like to develop my skills for the camera. At present I'm in a period of reflection and reassessment, and in the process of deciding on my own terms of engagement.

Liev Schreiber

Liev Schreiber was born in 1967 in San Francisco, California, but grew up in New York. A graduate of the Yale School of Drama, Schreiber also studied at the Royal Academy of Dramatic Art in London. He recently starred as Hamlet in the Public Theater's production of *Hamlet* (1999) in New York, directed by Andrei Serban. His other stage credits include *In the Summer House* (1993), *The Tempest* (1995), *All For One* (1993), *Goodnight Desdemona, Good Morning Juliet* (1992), *Escape From Happiness* (1992), *The Real Thing* (1991), *Richard III* (1991), *Underground* (1991), *The Size of the World* (1991), *Ivanov* (1990), *Macbeth* (1998) and *Cymbeline* (1998), for which he won both the Obie (off-Broadway) and Callaway Awards. His most recent stage appearance was in *Betrayal* on Broadway, directed by David Leveaux, with Juliette Binoche and John Slattery (2000). His screen credits include the Golden Globe-nominated film *Hurricane* (2000), *A Walk on the Moon* (1999), *Hamlet* (2000), *Jakob the Liar* (1999), the *Scream* trilogy (1996–2000), *Phantoms* (1998), *Sphere* (1998), *Twilight* (1998), *Ransom* (1996), *Walking and Talking* (1996), *Big Night* (1996), *Party Girl* (1995), *The Day Trippers* (1996), *Mad Love* (1995), *Denise Calls Up* (1996) and *Mixed Nuts* (1995). He starred in the film *Spring Forward* (2001), which he also co-produced. Schreiber was an Emmy and Golden Globe nominee for his lead role as Orson Welles in HBO's (Home Box Office television network) *RKO 281* (2000).

How did you come to be an actor and do you see yourself as specializing in a particular acting technique?
I think, like most kids, I came to acting through reading Shakespeare aloud in English class. I think I always had a thing for language, especially verse, and as my father was an actor, I was curious. When I went on to Hampshire College, I did not think it made sense just to study acting, so I did theatre on the side and studied semiotics, visual literacy and media studies.

I took a year abroad and studied at the Royal Academy of Dramatic Art in London, where I enjoyed learning stage combat and how to speak verse. I very much liked the pragmatism of English actor training. In

Europe, the arts are subsidized more than in America and, because of that, it is easier for theatres that produce classical plays to stay afloat. Therefore, classically trained actors can actually find work.

Initially I was very enamoured of the pragmatic approach towards classical training because it focused on technique, and technique was the thing I knew I had; I knew that I understood text, I had a musical ear and I could find the irony in things. European training, particularly English training, is based primarily on irony; irony is endlessly theatrical and a great way to approach a text. In America, textual analysis is more focused on character, but there are two ways to skin a cat. You can arrive at the same destination either way; it's just that I find that one way is more entertaining than the other.

You then went on to study at Yale. How did the Yale training vary from what you learned at RADA in London?
In England, there was no hiding from the fact that it took particular muscles to do the work. If you did not develop those muscles, you were not going to get by on charm.

Can you get by on charm in America?
The reality is that an actor needs to develop the skills that are going to get him employed. At the end of the day it is also a job that hopefully can support us. Unfortunately, nowadays we are led to believe that charm goes a lot further than technique, especially in the American film and television industry.

Does Method acting have any bearing on your technique?
As far as I know, the Method was Lee Strasberg's way of helping actors find a certain kind of emotional truth and source memory with which to inform text. I think this kind of acting lends itself very well to the ultra-naturalistic medium of film; hence its popularity in the States. Like everything in acting, I believe it is just a tool that one uses when appropriate. For instance, there is a whole world of plays (pre-Freud) that do not lend themselves so easily to this approach. I think a good actor mixes and matches from a wide range of tools in approaching text. Training is merely about increasing that supply of tools and thereby one's range; and then, of course, you should never discount instinct, which I think is the foundation of acting.

I am particularly interested in unconscious memory; I have trouble remembering things, but that does not mean I have not absorbed them unconsciously. Once in a while someone will tell me something that feels familiar, not intellectually, but somehow viscerally. My synapses may not be firing as well as they were when I was seven years old, but my unconscious memory is often engaged by seeing a certain colour or smelling a particular smell. That sensation is very difficult to describe; it is one of those things that can only be felt. The ambiguity or arbitrariness of it is what makes it human and therefore interesting. In other words, I do not need an explanation for the impulse; its source makes it interesting. An actor has a number of impulses that may or may not have anything to do with the narrative of a play but are somehow connected to that actor's unconscious and personal experience of the text. Using these unconscious impulses, along with basic text analysis, more or less describes how I work. I try to uncover what the unconscious memory is telling me about the text. Accessing unconscious memory is the thing that makes people laugh. It gets us out of our analytical heads and into a more visceral experience of the play.

How do today's audiences relate to a play like Hamlet, *the title role of which you played at the Public Theater in New York?*
There isn't a play more profoundly about humanity, and more generous towards humanity, than *Hamlet*; it is a miracle to me that a human could be capable of writing it because it is so directly about the human condition. Nowadays, people do not read enough or spend enough time with themselves to access those feelings, so the only way of shortening that distance between the audience and the play is through abstractions. Abstractions are related to unconscious memories; when the brain is functioning in an analytical way, a person is not involved in what they are watching on stage, but when something happens on stage that evokes an unconscious memory, suddenly that person forgets they are in the theatre. In the best of all situations, they get lost in themselves in relation to the play and have an unconscious memory event, like 'Oh, my God, my grandmother died last year'. From that point onwards, they begin to experience the play. The wonderful thing is that they do not explicitly think 'Oh, my God, my grandmother died last year', but simply, 'Oh, my God'. They do not necessarily make the connection, but something in them has become involved in a deeper way.

Shakespeare is good at engendering such connections because his plays are written in verse, and verse has a way of entering the subconscious mind. Speaking about acting Shakespeare, the director Andrei Serban said (as Peter Brook said before him, I think) that the audience is only going to understand about a fifth of what you say, so your job as an actor is to better that fraction. I believe that although people will probably only understand a fifth of what is being said *during* the performance, by the time the play has ended they will take about three or four fifths away with them. They do not know they have this amount, but in the course of their lives those elements will manifest themselves.

Would you be less happy playing a Shakespearean character like Falstaff, who is driven by prose, than a verse-speaking character like Hamlet?
Even without the formal structure of iambic pentameter, there are so many language elements driving prose text. I think there are just as many challenges and nuances in the prose speeches.

Do you approach Shakespearean prose as if it were verse?
I do not play prose and verse very differently. If you follow the clues in the text, the difference between the two tends to play itself.

Do you wish you could take more control over a performance?
The answer to this question is related to how I approach character research: you study everything as diligently as you can and then forget it all, because in the end it does not really matter. However, I read all the books I can lay my hands on because you never know when a piece of research might inform you; it's a process I go through partly out of neurosis and partly because I care about my role. The ultimate aim is to try to exert as much control as I possibly can throughout the process until the run begins, because you cannot control a performance in the same way as in rehearsal. I try to control all the elements for as long as possible, because ultimately you have to let go of it.

I think actors tend to associate text work with a kind of 'control' the writer is exerting on them, but in fact, it is the opposite. For me, text work opens up the possibilities of expression that I may not have known were there. Maybe I am just one of those people who responds to rhythm in language. There is something about it that is primitive and frees me from the 'control' of my analytical mind.

What do you think about reviews?
They are opinions, nothing more, but I happen to like hearing other

people's opinions, so I read them. I would not recommend that for most actors, though; I think it is difficult for some actors to separate the professional from the personal.

Do you feel the same about film criticism, when you are reading about yourself some eighteen months after the experience of making the film?
It is the same thing. Seeing the film eighteen months later is a unique experience in itself because often you are not in every scene and have never seen the whole thing with music and editing, etc. Seeing the finished product is a completely different experience from playing the scenes during the shooting. There is so much involved in a film above and beyond your work that when it is finally assembled it can be very different from how you imagined it. Because of this, I tend to feel less connected to films when they come out. I enjoy that. It's almost like seeing something you didn't know you were in.

How do you prepare to go on stage or in front of a camera?
For film, I tend to work physically first, whereas for theatre, I tend to work a little more analytically. I find that thinking gets me in trouble on film and emoting gets me in trouble on stage, perhaps because film seems to lend itself to behaviour whereas theatre lends itself to action. The truth is that most directors want behaviour, it is just that in theatre they want *better* behaviour. Brecht once said that at any given moment an actor is three things: the character that he or she is playing, the actor playing the character and a member of a socio-political society. I think this is a wonderfully liberating statement: it is a way of allowing myself access to audiences and to material. Also, it implies that there is generosity and compassion involved in acting. In a sense, it is the actor's responsibility to be *present*, rather than just a *represent*ative. I thrive on the idea of being present and accounted for.

Michael Sheen

Born in 1969 in Newport, Wales, Michael Sheen trained at the Royal Academy of Dramatic Art (RADA) in London, where he won the Laurence Olivier Bursary and launched straight into a West End début with *When She Danced*, playing opposite Vanessa Redgrave, in 1991. In 1993 he was nominated for the Ian Charleson Award for his performance in *Don't Fool with Love* with the Cheek By Jowl company and played the role of Fred in the world première of Harold Pinter's *Moonlight* at the Almeida (1993). In 1994 he played the title role in *Peer Gynt* in Ninagawa's production in Oslo, Tokyo and London, and in 1996–7 he played Lenny in Pinter's *The Homecoming* at the Royal National Theatre. He played the title role in Ron Daniels' production of *Henry V* for the Royal Shakespeare Company (1997) and took the role of Mozart in Peter Schaffer's *Amadeus* on Broadway (1999). His screen credits include the leading role in *Gallowglass* (1993), a three-part serial for the BBC, Stephen Frears's *Mary Reilly* (1996), *Wilde* (1997), with Stephen Fry, and Oliver Parker's *Othello* (1995). His most recent film project was *Four Feathers*, directed by Shekhar Kapur (2000).

What was your training as an actor, and do you specialize in any particular acting style?
I spent three years at RADA, but I think an actor's overall training begins when he or she starts acting. I did school plays and attended a brilliant youth theatre at home in West Glamorgan. I think of that as my first real training. I started there when I was about fourteen and I left when I was twenty-one. I did seven years at that youth theatre and it was a tremendously formative experience, both personally and as an actor. I also performed with the National Youth Theatre and tried to do as much as I possibly could before I went to drama school.

I do not think I specialize in a certain type of acting, but people who have seen the work I have done so far would probably describe it in a particular way. I like the idea of being able to adapt to as many different ways of telling stories as possible. One thing that is common to everything I have done is that it has all been quite physical. I do not necessarily mean physical in the sense of Theatre de Complicite, but in terms of trying to bring a physical presence to what I do. In Britain, acting is seen as very technical, text based and vocally based, whereas in America acting is seen as very emotional, intuitive and perhaps more physical. I enjoy trying to become as technically proficient as possible while keeping intuitive and physical.

From what does your interest in the physical side of acting stem?
I have always been a physical person. I have always enjoyed playing sports and the first thing I wanted to be was a football player. When I started acting seriously, I always had the option of expressing a story physically. In some ways, my acting style is quite extreme. There was never a moment when it occurred to me to think physically about acting, but I think I was inspired to use my body by a teacher at RADA called Ben Benison, who came from a very physical background, a combination of tap-dancing and Keith Johnstone's Theatresports improvisation company. He worked with us on improvisation. You never knew what you were going to do when you went into his classes, but at the same time he had a very definite set of beliefs about performance. It was quite a scary class because you had to take risks, but it was also enjoyable because of his personality. In fact, a lot of what I consider as my method of working was honed or influenced by the stuff we did with Ben.

Most of the work you do is in text-based theatre. What is the role of improvisation in your process of preparation for these types of roles?
The director Roger Michell thinks it is a good idea to improvise anything that is mentioned in the text that you do not actually see in the play. I agree with him, as this technique helps you to develop an actual physical memory of the scene as you are describing it on stage. The director Declan Donnellan also uses improvisation in a creative way. He asks you to put a scene into your own words, which is frightening to do but can be very useful. He often asks you to use the actual text from the play, but to improvise around it and try it different ways. His method is more about keeping the sense of improvisation without necessarily coming up with your own words and I try to carry this spirit of improvisation on stage to every performance. It is not that I try to do wildly different things every night, but that I keep that sense of inventiveness and freedom within a very particular structure. You need the spirit of inventiveness to give a performance that spark of life within the structure of the text and the scenes that you have worked on in rehearsal.

To what extent do you see yourself as your own director? You have directed plays yourself on occasion. Do you ever put your directorial skills into play as an actor?

Directors and producers have told me I should direct, and I have done on occasion. I always thought that developing a director's eye is just a normal part of being an actor; it is just the way I look at things and it can be both a good and a bad quality in an actor. The good thing is that I have an overview of the whole show and I can be aware of what is happening beyond my own role as opposed to just being totally submerged in what I am doing. However, coming out of what I am doing can be risky, so I have had to cultivate my awareness of what is going on alongside being in the moment with the character. Over the years, I have become less interested in myself as an actor within a show and more interested in the piece as a whole.

Are you ever tempted to direct the other actors in a play you yourself are acting in?

No. Unless you are the director, there is very little you can do. You get into real trouble if you start telling people what to do as an actor. If I am playing a leading part such as Henry V or Jimmy Porter in *Look Back in Anger*, I have a large influence on what the other actors are doing, because they are reacting off my character.

Henry V is a very good example: you come on, do a big speech and then go off again. There are not many opportunities to act with other people in real scenes, but from the beginning, I knew I wanted to underplay some of the rhetoric and speechifying. I spent a lot of time in rehearsals looking for ways in which I could involve other actors on stage, trying to make sure that no one was just standing there, holding a spear. I tried to get everyone really involved and I like to think that it helped other people in the play to have a more satisfying experience, because the speeches became scenes. For me, it was brilliant because it enabled me to respond to people, even though I was speaking all the time. Playing characters who do a lot of talking, like Jimmy Porter, you have to find out what you are responding to all the time. Although I do not direct the other actors in any way, I do quite heavily influence how other characters respond to me.

Actors fall into two groups. There are actors who work quite slowly and put off making choices for a quite a while; things simmer inside them and slowly, towards the end of the process, their choices emerge.

Then there are actors, such as me, who make a choice very quickly, throw it away and make another one immediately. I enjoy trying as many things as possible. You might make a particular choice for the beginning of the scene and then something else when you go over it again before the director makes a suggestion. When I have worked as a director, I have preferred directing the second kind of actor, because it seems a more collaborative process than working with an actor whose choices do not emerge for a long time. It does not necessarily mean that the performance is going to be any better or worse, though.

How important is the sense of ensemble in what you do?
Everything you do on stage has to have the ethos of an ensemble. A really good example of that for me was when I did *Look Back in Anger*. Jimmy Porter is a huge, dominating character who literally does not stop speaking and the other characters on stage basically have to just stand there, listening to him. It worked as an ensemble piece more than any other play I have ever done because we were a great company of actors. We communicated with each other very well and there were no egos getting in the way.

In terms of my own survival in the role of Jimmy, I knew I had to stop the audience from getting bored by listening to me talking all the time, so I decided to make my monologues seem like dialogues. It was important for the audience to see who and what Jimmy was responding to and I think anybody who talks that much is defending themselves. Then I had to work out what he was defending himself against. My take on Jimmy is that he feels he is constantly under attack; he even regards silence as a form of attack. Out of that reading came a sense of drama; not just an actor doing speeches. Even though the play is very textual, I think the production felt different because the other characters were just as important as Jimmy in the audience's imagination, telling the story through silence and gesture. If a play is fully explored, every actor on stage makes an equal contribution and it becomes ensemble theatre rather than just a vehicle for some star.

Do you think, having spent some time in America, that there is lots more star-vehicle theatre in the USA?
The British and American theatre industries suffer equally from the pressures of commercial success. The financial pressures have completely perverted mainstream theatre on both sides of the Atlantic.

Acting on a Broadway stage is the same as acting in the West End; the difference is so minimal as to be totally irrelevant. You are working for a management whose primary motivation is to make a financial success and, aside from the core middle-class audience, you are playing to an audience who is transient and usually touristy. It is a disembodied experience in some ways and you spend your time preaching to the converted. One of the major questions that people in the theatre community have to address is about audiences: why are you doing what you are doing and who is it you are doing it for? You cannot teach anyone anything through theatre; at best you can only reveal or share. I think sharing is the highest aspiration you can seek.

Is that how you would describe your relationship with the audience?
I think so. I think my relationship with the audience has changed over the years and it will keep changing. At the moment, I feel like the most you can hope for is to share and you have to be open and vulnerable to do this. When you work on something, you come to love it and feel that it is important; it comes to mean a lot to you. Then you go on stage and have to give something that means a lot to you to the audience. A lot of the time, the audience does not feel the same as you do. If you think the audience does not understand what you are doing, you start to close up, stop giving as fully as you should and then the performance dies. The hardest thing to do is to keep the channel open for any member of the audience to have the opportunity of sharing with you.

It is really difficult to play to the mass audience of mainstream theatre in some ways because they are not as interested in extremes or anything that is slightly distressing, confrontational or challenging. However, it can be the best audience to play to for that very reason, because what is the point of playing to an audience that is not going to be challenged by what you do? In one way, it is great to perform to an audience who understand everything you do and think it is fantastic and you don't really want to be playing to an audience full of people who say, 'I thought that was disgusting!' Ultimately, though, who are you going to affect the most?

How do you measure audience response? After all, most of the time, it is only the same few London critics who ever write about your performances. Are you attuned to the audience while you are up on stage?
On the most fundamental level, you develop an ability to sense what is

going on. There is a frequency that you tune in to and it is literally in the air, a channel between the audience and you. You either meet them there or you do not, but if you can get on to that frequency, you suddenly realize you can feel the audience there. When you are in tune with how the audience is feeling and where they are going, you can play with their emotions. That is the ideal state for acting.

Do you think of the critic as another audience member?
The critic is not just another audience member, but someone who sees a lot of theatre. I might not agree with their tastes particularly, but I have very rarely, if ever, read a review that has not made me think. You have to take what the critics say on board. Sometimes reading a review can be devastating, but I ask myself if I can incorporate any of it into my performance. If I try it and it works, then I have got better, but if it does not, I try something else. You might be upset by what you read, but in the long run it can only help you.

What are the most productive rehearsal conditions for you to work in?
It depends very much on the project. In some ways I think it would be great to have a really long rehearsal period, such as in Russia. I spoke to some actors at the Maly Theatre in St Petersburg who were just about to perform an adaptation of a Dostoyevsky novel. They had been rehearsing it for six months or maybe even a year, and had adapted every single moment from the novel. The first run-through they did went on for about twelve hours and then they just cut it down to size. If that version did not work, they would include different material and cut out other things. They moved things around like a jigsaw puzzle until they got what they wanted. That way of working is an incredible luxury. It is not necessarily a good way of doing things, but it would be nice to have the choice. With other projects, it may be better to have just four weeks to get it on. I certainly felt that with *Look Back in Anger*; if we had had any longer, it would not have felt right, and in any case, you learn the most by getting out in front of an audience.

What have you learned from mainstream theatre?
Mainstream theatre is mainstream theatre because it works on lots of different levels and reaches lots of people. I want to find out why that is and how to do it. It is dangerous to say 'I am going to turn my back on commercial theatre and do something very small and meaningful',

because you end up wondering why nobody is coming to see it. If you get the opportunity to do something different and you mess it up, you may not get that opportunity again. I intend to learn as much as I can from commercial theatre and find out why people respond to it, so when my opportunity comes to do something different, I will be prepared.

I have done well in mainstream theatre. You keep going at something until you are completely dissatisfied with it and then you move on. I am not totally dissatisfied yet; I am still developing and I can still get a lot out of it personally as an actor. It has given me opportunity and choice, but this can be a dangerous game, because by the time you are in a position to have enough choice, you need to remember why you got into acting in the first place. Take the example of the actor who says they do Hollywood films in order to finance their theatre work. The more empty blockbusters they do to finance their artistic projects, the more they compromise themselves. There is only so much of that you can do before you will not come back to the art any more.

Can you imagine yourself doing anything else?
I have to act. I can see myself doing other things as well but I can see that eventually I will have to get out of the situation I am in at the moment. Acting in mainstream theatre has been fine, but I cannot see myself continuing in the same way for the rest of my life.

How do you build a character?
I am mostly interested in playing extreme characters. In real life, the majority of people would not be able to bear being in the same room as some of the characters I have played, like Jimmy Porter and Mozart. When I act, I try to tell two stories at the same time, to dislocate the head from the heart. You tell one story to the head and another story to the heart and they are in conflict. If the character is complicated and the form of the story is fairly simple and accessible, then the audience is more likely to sympathize with the character. When the audience does not have to grapple with the form of a difficult play, they can engage with the characters more readily.

Let us take the example of Mozart. The surface story is about someone who is incredibly over-confident, arrogant, bratty, scatological, silly and obscene; if you were in a room with Mozart, you would be inclined to see this side of him alone. The story underneath is about someone who has a totally dependent relationship with his father, who is totally insecure, vulnerable and frightened of being on his own. He cannot understand why people do not like him and he is emotionally stunted because he has been a star since he was four. The more you can play the two sides off against each other, the greater the effect of dislocation upon the audience. The part of us that just cannot help being judgemental engages with the surface story, while the story underneath keeps undermining that judgement. However, as soon as you start engaging with the story underneath and becoming sympathetic towards the character, the surface story kicks in and you no longer feel sympathy. The two-way conflict for the audience keeps them engaged and creates a character's psychological truth.

Personality is to some degree a defence mechanism. It is not an expression of our true selves, it is rather a defence against our true selves. The conflict is there in order to allow you to survive in the world, but in the long run it will destroy you. As an audience member, you watch a character moving through time with this conflict within them. You understand why they have that conflict and you can see it is going to destroy them unless they change. That is what allows you to engage with the character. If they change, then it is a happy story; if they do not change, then it is a tragic story. Either way, an audience member comes away with a greater knowledge of the character and, if they are willing to open themselves up to it, of themselves.

Do you undertake lots of research for a production?
Research is about what you do in the rehearsal room and letting the text work imaginatively on you. Mike Nichols says that the down-time, when you are not working on something, is usually the most productive time, because you let go of the idea of coming up with answers and suddenly things start to appear; suddenly you begin to discover things. You need to spend a lot of time developing ways of making your subconscious come up with ideas.

Beyond that, acting is all about getting out there and doing it. It is about playing the scene and trying something different and playing it again. You have to be as exploratory as possible and doing that requires all your technique, heart, soul, emotion and courage. It is really frightening because you have to be prepared to look like a complete idiot in front of your fellow actors.

You can come up with any excuse to defend yourself from something that is frightening, but ultimately there is no defence. In order to get to the good stuff, you have to go through the frightening part. You simply have to get on with it, so that whenever you need to do it in the future, you can do it quickly. Needing lots of time and apparatus to act can be a dangerous crutch. Personally, I have seen too many people mystifying the acting process to cover their own fears, but ultimately you should have it all in you already. Each one of us walks around as a mini-version of the whole universe; everything we need is inside us. If you can access that, and access it in other people, then that is when the fireworks go off.

Antony Sher

Antony Sher is an actor, writer and artist. He was born in South Africa and at the age of nineteen moved to England, where he trained at the Webber Douglas Academy. His many theatre appearances include, for the Royal National Theatre, *Stanley* (1996), for which he won the Laurence Olivier Best Actor Award, *Uncle Vanya* (1992), *The Resistible Rise of Arturo Ui* (1991) and *Titus Andronicus* (1995). Other work includes *Torch Song Trilogy* (1985), for which he also won the Laurence Olivier Best Actor Award. His work for the Royal Shakespeare Company includes *Richard III* (1984, four major awards, including Evening Standard Best Actor Award), *The Merchant of Venice* (1987), *Tamburlaine* (1992), *Cyrano* (1997), *The Winter's Tale* (1999) and *Macbeth* (1999). Television credits include *The History Man* and *Genghis Cohen*. Films include *Mrs Brown* (Evening Standard Peter Sellars Award) and *Live and Kicking*. He has written both fiction and non-fiction, and his books on acting are *The Year of the King* and *Woza Shakespeare!* (co-written with his partner, Gregory Doran). His autobiography, *Beside Myself*, was published by Hutchinson in 2001. His art work has been exhibited in Stratford, the Barbican and the Royal National Theatre. In 2000 he was knighted for his services to acting and writing.

What was your training as an actor?

My early theatrical experiences were in South Africa during my school years. I had a private teacher called Esther Caplan, who was a deliciously outrageous character and, perhaps surprisingly for her generation, was interested in modern drama and modern acting skills: it was through her that I learned about Arnold Wesker and his contemporaries, about Method acting and improvisation. There was a yearly eisteddfod (an arts festival) in Cape Town and I performed speeches and duologues. My first taste of audience laughter came in a school production, playing the Brian Rix part in a Whitehall farce.

South African theatre in the 1950s and 1960s was conservative and anodyne, and censorship prevented performances by avant-garde writers such as Wesker and Pinter, but I saw the première of Athol Fugard's *Hello and Goodbye*, which made an enormous impression on me. Fugard played the leading role, a part I played myself years later. It was a play about a poor, white family, was quite different from anything I'd seen before and presented a fascinating alternative to the homogeneity of everything else on the stage. After school, I had to do national service in the South African army and I left for England in 1968, beguiled by my parents' exotic description of 'overseas'. The choice of careers for me was between fine art and acting. I chose acting and enrolled at the Webber Douglas Academy. I couldn't find work after I'd qualified, but won a scholarship on a postgraduate acting course at the Stables Theatre, which was co-run by Granada Television, Manchester Polytechnic and Manchester University.

Do you specialize in a particular technique?
My acting technique changes all the time and to keep fresh and vital it has to keep changing and growing. Acting is only your view of other human beings. It's fatally easy to sit back on your talent and stop growing – that's what happened to someone like, say, Richard Burton – and I work hard on myself to prevent sterility. I keep fresh by feeding my curiosity and by keeping alert to possibilities on stage. During the course of my career I've worked with performers who've inspired me to act 'in the moment' and I've learned a great deal from observing and working alongside other actors. Jonathan Pryce was an early inspiration: for my first professional job, I acted with him in *King Lear* (1973) at the Liverpool Everyman Theatre. He played Edgar and I played the Fool. At that time my own acting was very precise, detailed and pre-planned. I noticed that Jonathan was able to find the essence of a scene and reinvent it from night to night; there were ways in which his performance was genuinely different each time and the experience of acting with him was one of danger, unpredictability and excitement. I remember one night in one of the heath scenes, he actually kicked me! It was an entirely new impulse and I realized that I had just been going through the motions of performance and that he was giving me a stark warning to 'wake up!' He was always alert to the moment. No matter how many times you play a character, you have to keep surprising yourself, the other actors and the audience. I'm currently playing Macbeth and I'm particularly conscious of this in the banquet scene when Banquo's ghost appears – I play it differently each time.

In recent years I've been very inspired by Fiona Shaw. I saw her in *Electra* and in *Hedda Gabler* and what stunned me was the recognition that she was going through a panoply of emotions *for real*. I realized that I had to investigate her approach and this encouraged me to experiment with techniques of emotional recall using memory and senses, and this is something I have drawn on at particular moments in particular performances.

How do you think of acting?
I think of it as a form of portraiture. Many argue that there are two types of actor: the personality actor who brings a part to themselves; and the character actor who travels away from themselves to become the part. I think the film industry prefers actors to be types, which is perhaps why I have not done a great deal of film. In *Sophie's Choice* Meryl Streep travelled away from herself to become Sophie; the personality actor works more internally and is not so interested in the outside. I started out as a character actor: I was fascinated by the idea of disguise, but these days I am much more interested in putting myself on the line. In Anthony Burgess's version of Rostand's *Cyrano de Bergerac*, the central character talks of his 'visible soul' and that's what I see in Fiona Shaw's acting; it's not just technique, it's about an attitude to life.

I do a lot of painting and drawing and always sketch the characters that I'm playing. My scripts have all sorts of drawings in the margins. After the production, I do a full-size portrait of the character that I've played. I couldn't draw Macbeth at all during rehearsals, which worried me at the time, but in retrospect I realize it's because I feel as though I am playing a mind, an imagination. If I were to draw him now, I'd draw a picture of a man wrestling with his own head, desperately trying to rid himself of dreadful visions.

What motivated you to act?
I grew up feeling a sense of 'otherness' in South Africa. I was conscious of my Jewishness in a society that was anti-semitic; and I was gay, though didn't really know it. South Africa was a macho, extrovert, rugby-playing environment and I didn't fit in at all. Acting provided me with a means of ridding myself of my shyness and becoming anyone I wanted to be. Now I am much more at peace, less absorbed by disguise and more interested in the 'visible soul'.

Are you aware of other influences on your acting?
As a young man I was very impressed with Olivier's film acting. When I

arrived in London in 1968, I caught his last stage performances in Strindberg's *The Dance of Death*, O'Neill's *Long Day's Journey into Night* and *The Merchant of Venice*, but in the flesh he was always disappointing to me. I never saw a performance that blew me away but his life and his legendary status are fascinating and inspiring. I greatly admired Alec Guinness and Peter Sellers, who both had an astonishing ability to become different people, whether comic or tragic. Comedy is something I now find difficult, which perhaps relates to life.

Do you undertake much research for your roles?
It's very important, I regard it as a wake-up call, and I do a lot. Much of what I strive for is to be alive to every moment, and acting can be like a dream or a sleep if one is not careful. The violence of a street fight can be shocking without many blows landing, and a fight on stage can be overly balletic and choreographed. Whenever I'm in a stage fight, I think about the blows that *hurt*.

For *Macbeth*, I was engaged in two levels of research: with the company and by myself. At the company level, the director asked us all to relate our most extreme experience of fear because every single character in the play feels intense fear at some point. At the personal level, I met up with two men who had committed murder and who had served their time in prison. They were probably amongst the most remarkable encounters I've had in my life: the first man was still haunted by his crime and the second was haunted by his punishment. The first man had stabbed his best friend and interrupted his attack to consider calling an ambulance, but then returned to finish the job. He knew as he was stabbing the other man that he was doing something he shouldn't, and this is true of Macbeth – before he commits the crime, he knows that it's wrong. There was something else about the two meetings which I found useful: when I asked them the questions 'Do you have nightmares?' 'Do you see your victim?', they both replied: 'Only when I'm awake.' Both had waking dreams when their victim would be close by, exuding calm and compassion. Before hearing their accounts, I'd found the scene of Banquo's ghost full of cliché; afterwards, I saw it differently and found a new energy in it.

When Greg Doran is directing me, I rely on him for his historical knowledge of Shakespeare. I'm less interested in historical research and more interested in how to speak and do Shakespeare. After twenty years working with many people at the Royal Shakespeare Company, I am only now starting to feel that I know how to do it. I've learned a great deal from the director John Barton and the voice coach Cicely Berry, and also by just doing Shakespeare.

Have you found verse speaking difficult?
The great difficulty of Shakespeare is how to speak it, and in places you have to hold a complex idea or image over many lines. Mark Rylance can achieve a real freshness of delivery with the most familiar of speeches. When I began at the Royal Shakespeare Company, I felt that I was the outsider, that I wasn't going to be allowed to be a success; after all, there weren't many leading actors who were Jewish and South African! I realized with time that everyone felt awed by the institution. With Richard III, I felt I had a strong visual sense of the character but was intimidated by the language. Initially I think I struggled too hard with the verse speaking. Cicely Berry talked about breathing and encouraged us to invent imagery for ourselves as we were speaking; it's a way of writing a freshness into the part for yourself. I also learned through doing other authors; Tourneur's verse is jagged and awkward like barbed wire, and Marlowe's lines are pounding and hard to vary. Coming back to Shakespeare seemed easier; in the manner of jazz musicians, he gets the beat going but then does all sorts of variations and at the same time creates an extraordinary psychological complexity. I find Tom Stoppard's plays present the same sort of linguistic challenges; speaking the lines in *Travesties* is a technical feat for an actor; unless you're deft with language, you get neither the meaning nor the laughs across to an audience.

Do you prepare mentally and physically for a part?
Mentally, I research by reading and by talking to the actors and the director in rehearsals. I'm actually pleased that I can now do a performance without articulating it exhaustively because I had a tendency to over-analyse. I've been acting Macbeth for three months and only just feel that I am starting to understand him. When I played Marlowe's Tamburlaine, I trained for six months. Terry Hands, the director, wanted to show the battles and fights and felt that Tamburlaine should be a superman, so I trained with Johnny Hutch, who had been a circus performer, appeared in music hall and worked on gymnastics with a theatre company called The Kosh. I climbed up ropes three or four times a week so that I could climb them in production and speak while

climbing. When I played Cyrano in Rostand's play I had to train in sword fighting for a couple of months. I felt that I needed to lose weight to play Macbeth, that he should be leaner and fitter than I was, so I worked out in a gym for six months.

I think there's also a question about emotional training and being able to tap into emotional memory. In *The Winter's Tale*, for example, Leontes undergoes sixteen years of grieving and repentance. I didn't want to play a 'saintly' Leontes; I felt that he should be emotionally naked, that the shock of seeing Hermione come alive should make his nerve endings show. I used to sit alone in the wings for twenty minutes before Act V, dredging up sadness – I thought about the death of my father, or anything which moved me, I tried to open emotions and access them on stage. I feel that the heart of Macbeth is his violent but glorious imagination, which allows him to see the consequences of his act before he does it. Despite the fact that he is a soldier and is used to killing, he experiences terrible hallucinations while killing Duncan. I see him as a man whose brain is hurting and burning, and as a man whose mind, as the line goes, 'is full of scorpions'.

What sort of rehearsal conditions are best for you?
Rehearsals change with every director; often they will adapt to you if you are the leading actor. I have been tempted to direct just to find out why so many directors do their work so badly, but I suppose from an actor's point of view their job looks easier. I think many actors have love–hate relationships with directors; we expect them to know everything but hate it when they tell us. The ideal director allows you creative involvement while overseeing the production. I could never work with a director who pre-planned everything because I need to work organically, but the other extreme of amorphous, under-energized rehearsals is also difficult. The work of the director is reinvented all the time; in a truly productive process, everyone should be working creatively. I find it tricky working with designers who have created the set and costumes before rehearsals begin because the character and the production evolve over time and fixing the process in that way can block creativity. Rehearsals must be a true investigation and not a prescribed map prepared by directors and designers.

Do you read reviews?
I've gone through phases of reading and not reading reviews. At the

moment I get what I call a temperature reading from friends or from my agent. They read all the reviews and mark them out of ten so that I have a sense of how a show has been received. Praise can be as destructive as criticism. I don't invite people along to give me feedback but I know directors who do and can see how they would find it useful. I do read reviews of other productions – in fact I read reviews of other shows addictively!

What are your aspirations as an actor?
I want to do more film and television work, and feel that because I am seen predominantly as a theatre actor I don't necessarily get offered as much film work as I would like. I used to have a list of stage roles that I wanted to do, but found that the desire to meet my own ambitions became too oppressive so I don't do that any more. I like to be surprised by offers.

Anna Deavere Smith

Anna Deavere Smith is an actor, writer and academic. She is known for her one-woman shows in which she transforms herself into a multitude of characters taken from real life. In her works, *Fires in the Mirror: Crown Heights Brooklyn and Other Identities* (New York Shakespeare Festival 1992, published by Doubleday), *Twilight: Los Angeles 1992* (The Mark Taper Forum 1993, published by Doubleday) and *House Arrest* (New York Shakespeare Festival, 2000), Smith explores notions of American identity. She is the author of *Talk to Me: Listening Between the Lines* (Random House, 2000), which explores the process of her work. She is a professor at New York University, appointed in the School of the Arts, with an affiliation with the NYU School of Law and the Center for Art and Public Policy. She is the founding director of the Institute on the Arts and Civic Dialogue, which is dedicated to finding new ways and forms for artists to create works pertaining to social issues. She is the recipient of a variety of honorary degrees and awards, among them the MacArthur 'Genius' Fellowship.

What was your training as an actor?
I trained classically in a three-year conservatory programme in San Francisco. The training was divided into two halves: one half focused on voice, speech, physical capability and text, while the other half emphasized psychological realism. It was a sort of watered-down version of the Method. After this initial training, I began to seek out my own methods and developed an acting technique based on listening to people's speech patterns and repeating what they said in the way that they said it, as an effort to learn the links between speech and identity. I took my cues from Shakespeare, who among his many gifts had the ability to capture character in the rhythms of speech and in the images that people spoke – as they spoke. Perhaps Shakespeare taught me how to listen for how people become themselves in speech. My grandfather told me when I was a girl, 'If you say a word often enough, it becomes you.' So my acting technique is a combination of Shakespeare and my grandfather, a twentieth-century American black man with an eighth-grade education. Aside from that, I also did

a lot of contact-improvisation-type training in New York, which helped me develop.

How would you define acting?
I will begin by defining acting in terms of what it is not: it is not *being*, although I was trained to believe that it was. I was trained to find the character within yourself and was taught that acting was equivalent to *existing on stage*, but now I believe that this leads to a spiritual dead end. Acting is really about building a bridge between the self and the other. As the critic Richard Schechner suggests, there's the 'not not'. This is the point where you are not yet the character, even though you are trying to be the character. There's also a point where you're no longer yourself. So you're not the character, and you're not yourself. You're in the 'not not' – which is a positive. I think this is the most we can hope for. I don't think we can really 'be' anybody else. The actor is a vehicle of consciousness, projected through a fictional character, and the fiction displays great truth. Acting is misunderstood in today's America; it is seen as something that lawyers and politicians do to project a persona.

What motivates you to act?
Curiosity about others motivates me to act. I like to know what it is like to be somebody else, to wear those pants or that dress and I enjoy the physical experience of being someone else. On stage, I feel less bound by the notion that I only have one representation of myself in the world. Acting provides the possibility of metaphor and it is a way of taking the audience to another place.

Which actors have exerted the strongest influence upon you?
Particular performances impress me all the time, as well as certain performers. I recently particularly enjoyed Eartha Kitt and Toni Collette's performances in *The Wild Party on Broadway* (2000). I love Elizabeth Taylor in *Who's Afraid of Virginia Woolf?* and Anthony Hopkins, Judi Dench and Lily Tomlin in *Tea with Mussolini*. I am intrigued by film and television performances, because when they are good I marvel at the specificity of choices that people make. And perhaps we really are approaching a kind of special time with those mediums. I think Irene Worth is a wonderful actress. Artists working in other arts have also on occasion greatly influenced me, such as the opera singer Jessye Norman. I love the music of the composer John Adams because it is profoundly emotional. I love

Picasso, and visit the Picasso Museum each time I go to Paris. He did so much more than document human beings – he showed us his vision of humans. This interests me, because I have sought to document humans in order to get to the truth of them. I am fascinated by Picasso's confidence in putting forth his vision as a way of pointing to a truth.

Why does television and film present such a challenge to you?
I did a film of my play *Twilight*, acted in the movie *The American President* and I have also done some television lately. On screen, it is difficult to feel the degree of freedom you feel on stage and create unique characters because you are confined by what you physically represent, but television and film are taking over the world. In fact, I am in a quandary over what to teach young actors these days. Given that most of them will end up with jobs in television and film, training for these media should be represented in their acting programmes. My recent experiences of working with stage actors in the Institute on Arts and Civic Dialogue have been very rewarding, but, personally speaking, I am more oriented towards television and film at present.

How much do you try to develop your acting skills?
The only way to do it properly is when I am actually performing, but when I am not on stage, I make notes and listen to people around me. Stanislavsky was the first person to get to the heart of the problem of how to hone your skills as an actor. One of the difficulties of training as an actor is that acting is a form that depends on other people; a dancer can go to a dance class whenever he or she wants to improve, a pianist can sit down at the piano and practice, but as an actor, I feel like I am right back to where I started every time I begin on a new project. There is no single class I could go to, to practise my skills – no single teacher. There never has been. I have to take a little from life, a little from art, a little from politics. I find that in watching public life, where people are performing in order to win position, I am learning what acting is not. This inspires me to commit to finding more and more truths about human beings, and using acting to find it.

Describe your research process.
I create plays in which I play many different characters. I tell a story with many differing viewpoints and build a picture of a large community, using only me. Most of the plays begin with an event, such as the

LA riots or the Crown Heights riots in Brooklyn. I begin by going into the community and carrying out interviews with hundreds of people. The interviews are about an hour long and I record them on a tape-recorder or a DAT (digital audio tape) machine. I did around 280 interviews for *Twilight* and over 400 for *House Arrest*. Then I listen to all the tapes, pick the most interesting parts from hours of material and narrow it down to about two or three hours' worth. Next, I learn the speech of the character by listening to a Walkman and repeating the words to myself over and over again, before a vocal coach comes in and helps me get the exact nuances, down to the pauses and the 'ums' and 'ahs'. It is useful to have the coach there to help me pinpoint the moments when what I am saying differs from what I am hearing. Getting this precise intonation provides an extraordinary key to the character, and in some ways the essence of characters is in their voice. The goal of the process is to create a character that isn't just a *sketch* of a Jewish person or a Hispanic person, but a detailed embodiment.

Aside from the character-development process, I do an enormous amount of background reading that is particularly heavy when I am researching well-known figures. Traditionally, when you prepare a role for the stage, you start with the text and then go and do whatever background research you need to do. But in my case, the research has to happen before the text is created on tape. For my last project, I had staff going out and amassing a huge amount of research on people, but ultimately, as a performer, I am only as good as the interview I get on tape.

How do you prepare mentally and physically for a performance?
Performing for three hours beyond my normal vocal range is extremely demanding and it requires a lot of adrenalin; the people I play on stage do things with their voices that are not good for my vocal cords. Then there is the intellectual demand of learning the text in all its minutiae; it is difficult to know a text in that amount of detail and maintain its freshness. There is also a physical challenge: if I am in a run, by 3 p.m. in the afternoon my non-play-related activities have more or less ceased and I try not to take phone calls after that time.

How do you prepare a role?
Typically, rehearsals begin four or five weeks before opening, with the director, designers, dramaturg – and sometimes dramaturgs – the acting coach, vocal coach and me present. Although the director would

normally bear the responsibility for delivering a show, in this case the responsibility is mine, because I am the author, because I have conceived of the method of work and, most importantly, because I feel a social responsibility to the characters I play. They are alive, after all, and frequently I have interviewed them about a controversial and possibly life-and-death event. How they appear is more than what they say. I also am committed to saying what they said, exactly as they said it. In this way, of all the figures involved in the production, I have the most intimate relationship to the characters. My acting coach has the next most intimate relationship to the characters. The characters, for all intents and purposes, and the act of bringing them alive, *are* the play, *are* the event. To prepare for a role, I have to be intimately involved in all aspects of gathering the information, putting it into a show, knowing what the stage world of the show is (the *mise en scène*) and ultimately delivering that show, each night, to an audience – some of whom may know the people I am portraying. If acting is creating a fiction to illuminate a truth – and I think it is – then my preparation calls for my being aware of all aspects of the creation of that fiction.

What was your most challenging performance?
They have all been very different. Although *Fires in the Mirror* was probably the simplest show I ever did, in some ways it was the hardest, because it was my first encounter with success and this brought with it some unexpected problems. I had to deal with losing my voice and I simply was not prepared to give so many performances and deal with an extended run. I learned a lot about my voice from this experience, such as finding out that I needed a vocal coach.

One of the most challenging pieces I did was with Alvin Alley Dance Company. I interviewed the dancers and composed a libretto from their voices that became the score to which the dancers performed. Their words were their music and I was speaking them on stage as they danced, so I had to get it perfect. I am not a dancer and I was always afraid that I would say something in the wrong place and it would upset the timing and position of the dancers' movements.

What director did you respond to most creatively?
All the directors I have worked with have brought different things to the table. When I did the film of *Twilight*, it was interesting to work with a cinematographer.

What do you think are the most productive rehearsal conditions?
I am still examining the rehearsal process and I have not really found a solution. I would like to feel less separated from the design team and I would like to spend several weeks working intensively on the speech alone with a vocal coach, and my acting coach, before formal rehearsals begin. I would like to deliver the play as performed rather than to deliver it as a script.

How do you build a relationship with the audience?
I am not sure, but on the best nights the conditions feel right: the audience and I are in the theatre for the same reason and the show works. On a macro level, I see my performance as a way of convening people around the idea of a more equitable American society. If I could speak in other languages, I would carry out this quest in other parts of the world.

The first thing I do if I want to discover something about the world is go to the audience. At interview stage, the interviewee is the actor and I am the audience. Then I become the analyst and playwright, before removing myself from society and going into rehearsals. Finally, I take the play back out into society, by performing the work on stage in front of an audience. I do not just want the community to hear *me* – I want to hear *them*.

The secret of performing lies in presence. Joseph Chaikin, the founder of the influential Open Theater in America, defined presence in *The Presence of the Actor* as feeling as if the actor on stage is standing next to you wherever you are in the audience. It is all about having a deep desire to connect and people come to the theatre because they too want to connect. The actor does not produce the connection alone, the audience has to push forward also; the two have to meet in the middle.

Are you drawn towards certain roles?
I am most interested in working with directors who love actors and will push me to learn more. As a writer, I want to work with actors who want to learn more. Whatever project I do, it has got to teach me something new.

Who are the most useful critics of your acting?
My coaches are the most useful critics of my acting because they understand my process. They also tend to be the toughest critics, and I have tried to surround myself with people who will be tough critics, specifically because they too are invested in the process. Other than that, I find

that people who are perceptive about human beings and about feelings are very useful critics. The film director Mike Nichols, for example, is someone who always has profoundly interesting things to say. I would love to have Lily Tomlin do a critique of my work. I always learn so much from watching her, and from listening to her. I do not find criticism or praise useful when it comes from people who have only seen a show once, and who presumably come for a variety of reasons. Serious criticism needs to be focused on a clearly understood, shared objective.

What are your aspirations as an actor?
I want to get better, aim for subtler performances and be more specific and alive in the moment. I want to be able to change on a dime and I admire certain performers on television and film very much for their ability to deliver a performance in a compressed amount of time. I still have to learn how to do this.

Do you have broad desires for the future of acting?
I would like to see actors rid themselves of stereotypes and my aim is to create a play featuring all kinds of different actors together. For instance, my new play involves a combination of Asian, Latino, white and black actors. I do not understand why people go to the theatre to see plays with actors of entirely the same colour and background who all have the same sensibility about the world. If only we could get beyond liking one thing at the expense of liking a lot of things.

People do not need actors to be 'real'. Stanislavsky wanted to find reality on the stage because what he saw were 'wooden, contrived' performances. He made an incredible contribution to the study of acting. Yet he was doing this in a time when, for example, psychoanalysis was taking off as a practice. He was also speaking to an audience he knew well.

At the end of the twentieth century, we find ourselves in a situation where we are not as interested in deep character study – we don't presume to know anyone well – nor do we seem to be committed to that. Psychoanalysis has gone the way of pharmaceutical intervention. Communities all over the world become increasingly complex. It's hard to know who you are performing for. It's not enough to be 'real' these days. And since acting should shed light – rather than simply mirror – I would say that the future of acting is precarious right now.

I do not know where the future of acting lies. Perhaps what we should be doing is something more Picassoesque – perhaps we should indicate to our audience that what they accept as real is not so real. Perhaps we should question the accuracy of the camera. Everything is so staged, even in everyday life, that we have a much bigger task than Stanislavsky had. He wanted to make the stage more believable. Perhaps we have to make life more believable. Perhaps we need to pick up that part of the actor's enterprise that has as much to do with philosophy, poetry and activism as it has to do with being mere replicas of what we see around us every day. Yet I don't know how realistic this is. We are living, in the Western world, in a time when amassing material wealth is so important to people, as is comfort. Jean-Paul Sartre suggests in one of his works that if we see an actor reading the financial pages, the pages should be upside-down. Now, most of us are reading the financial pages right side up. The pursuit of property prevails as a goal, and yet I think an actor is so much more than property. An actor is the light inside the property, shedding light on all the places that are barren as well as the places that are glorious.

We have a spiritual problem; and in some societies, I can imagine it might even be considered an ethical one. Success in our world is measured by the degree to which we are firmly planted at the centre of things, yet so many things in the history of art have suggested that we artists belong not in the centre but somewhere on the outskirts, and that our job is to reflect on the centre from that position. We're faced with an interesting dilemma.

Elaine Stritch

Born in 1926 in Michigan, Elaine Stritch made her name on Broadway and in the West End in such musicals as the revivals of Rogers and Hart's *Pal Joey* (1952) and *On Your Toes* (1954) and the original productions of Noël Coward's *Sail Away* (1961) – which Coward wrote specifically for Stritch – and Stephen Sondheim's *Company* (1970). Stritch first visited England with *Sail Away* in 1961 and returned to the UK with Hal Prince's production of *Company* ten years later. Taking up residence in the country for thirteen years from 1972, Stritch co-starred with Donald Sinden in the television series *Two's Company* (London Weekend Television, 1975–9) and acted in the West End productions of Tennessee Williams's *Small Craft Warnings* (1974) and Neil Simon's *Gingerbread Lady* (1976). In 1985 she returned to New York, taking the role of Parthy in the Tony Award-winning revival of *Show Boat* on Broadway (1994) and the Tony Award-nominated production of Edward Albee's *A Delicate Balance* (1995). Her film credits include *Cocoon: The Return* (1988), Woody Allen's *September* (1987), *Out to Sea* (1997), *Krippendorf's Tribe* (1998), *Foolproof* (2000) and *Autumn in New York* (2000). Her television credits include a recurring role in *Law and Order*, for which she won an Emmy Award (America's most prestigious television accolade), *An Inconvenient Woman* (for which she was nominated for an Emmy Award), *The Cosby Show*, *An Unexpected Life*, *Third Rock from the Sun*, *Oz* and *Soul Man*. Stritch was inducted into the Theater Hall of Fame in 1995.

What was your training as an actor and do you practise any particular technique?
I think life is a pretty good technique for acting and I resort to it, naturally, to help me with every single thing I do in the theatre. I do not know if there is actually a technique of acting, but there is a discipline: acting classes, singing classes, dancing classes; keeping in shape in every department is necessary to enhance your natural God-given talent. Noël Coward described the technique of acting as 'Learn your lines and don't bump into the furniture'. Well, Noël, not quite! However, there is more truth than poetry in what he said. Look, the way I see it, tell the

audience what the author's trying to say to them and listen to your director. If the director isn't any good, do not listen to him, but look like you are; if you are a good actor, you will get away with it.

I studied at the Dramatic Workshop at the New School for Social Research in Greenwich Village, New York, alongside Marlon Brando, Walter Matthau, Tony Curtis, Rod Steiger and the Lunts (a famous comedic couple). When you arrive in New York aged seventeen from some Midwestern city such as Michigan, you think, 'Social research – what the hell is that?'

We studied Stanislavsky, who rightly said that as an actor you do not do anything without a good reason. It was quite a shock, but the son of a gun was right. Stanislavsky was all about reality with a capital 'R' and motivation with a capital 'M'. There was no posing; every thing, every word and every move had to be straightforward and on the level; in other words, no bullshit. What is your motivation? Why are you angry with your mother? Where do you stand on the stage to express this anger? I remember once Harold Clurman, who directed me in William Inge's *Bus Stop* (1956), had us reading the play over and over for two weeks out of a four-week rehearsal period. Nobody was allowed to get on their feet for two weeks, but when we did get up – surprise, surprise – we seemed to know what we were doing without having to put up with any of that laborious stage blocking. If you really understand the play, your part in it sort of stages itself. Clurman had a very strong belief in this. Actually, there was very little staging to deal with in my part as Grace, the owner of the diner, because I was behind the counter for two-thirds of the play. One day, I asked Clurman if I could come out from behind my counter somewhere in the first act because I was getting kind of antsy back there. He said, 'Sure.' I said, 'When?' He said, 'When you feel like it.' I knew I had to pick the right moment so as to avoid distracting attention from the other actors. In one run-through, Kim Stanley forgot to pick up her coffee cup from the counter, so I took it to her table, stage right. This was entirely acceptable to Clurman, who said, 'Keep it in, Elaine, exactly that way.' An actor should always do it for real; I think good actors actually find it too embarrassing to fake it.

I was never an actual member of Lee Strasberg's Actors' Studio, the home of Method acting, but I was invited as a guest on one occasion. I had done a couple of Broadway shows and was beginning to cut my teeth, so to speak. Strasberg came up to me before the class started and said, 'What are you doing here?', to which I replied, 'You invited me.' He laughed, gave me a hug (which was not like him at all, so I had heard) and said, 'Elaine, you are very welcome here, but you do not need to study the Method; you were born with it.' I did not realize at the time what a great compliment that was. 'Some are born great, some achieve greatness and some have greatness thrust upon them.' As far as so-called Method acting is concerned, I guess I'm in category one – according to Lee Strasberg, anyway, and that ain't bad!

Speaking of Method acting, if an actor feels a lack of truth creeping in, it is always because of fear. I have fought fear all my life, sometimes with phoney-baloney help (out of a bottle) which actually feeds the fear, and that's no good, or by hanging in till you have licked it. I settled for the latter in 1987.

You lived in London for many years. Did you find performing in the UK different from performing in America?
I do not think audiences differ so much as a rule. The only difference between audiences as far as I am concerned is good audiences and bad audiences, and far worse than either of those is no audience at all.

How would you describe the difference between singing and acting? Is performing in a musical different from performing a dramatic play?
Singing is acting in flight, but you have to make sure that the acting stays with you after the take-off or you will crash-land. For me, performing in a musical is much harder than doing a straight play because your vocal cords take on a double duty. Doing eight shows a week is not only emotionally exhausting, but physically tiring as well. You have to train like an Olympic athlete. I do not know what kind of voice I have, but when I sing a song, I make sure I tell a story and I have been told it reaches people. What I do know is, 'I got rhythm, I got music and who could ask for anything more?'

Do you prefer straight plays to musicals?
Either, or: the part is what matters. If the part is good, I do not care whether the characters sing or dance or neither. Musicals are harder than straight plays because you have to look after your physical condition so carefully. Usually musical plays are comedies and comedies are a lot harder and more stressful to play than serious parts. As Neil Simon says, 'Dying is easy, comedy is hard.' You either have it or you don't, but

if you don't have it, you will not even be able to do dramatic parts. I think an actor with no sense of humour should try something else.

Do you find it difficult to move between live performance and film?
No, I do not. Maybe I am oversimplifying, but acting for film is just getting out in front of a camera instead of a theatre audience. When I do a film, I pretend that all the camera operators, the director, everybody in make-up and wardrobe, the caterers, the producer and the backers (if they unfortunately happen to be visiting the set) are my audience; they inspire me to perform just like the audience in a theatre in New York. There is a lot of waiting involved in movies. I hate that element and call it 'trailer time'. Watch television? Too distracting. Take a nap? Forget about it, unless you want to re-do hair and make-up. Japanese pillows do not work for me, not the way I nap. I guess the smart thing to do is get bigger parts and stay out of your trailer.

What motivates you to act?
It sort of offends me to get all analytical about acting because of the fact that it comes so naturally to me. However, in answer to your question, my answer is to escape from reality: Make believing/ Is highly appealing/ To me!

Acting is a game of pretending: you're not you, you are someone else; someone far more interesting, exciting and dramatic. That's the ticket. Let me tell you something: due to a lot of hard work, I have very recently discovered, in this, the autumn of my life, that there is no-one more interesting or more exciting or more dramatic than me. I think, thank God, I'm experiencing a bit of maturity, self-worth and all that jazz.

When you finish a performance, do you return to yourself, or does the character stay with you off-stage?
I am afraid Elaine goes everywhere with me, on-stage and off, and I just can't seem to shake her. In the autumn of 2001, when I do my own show – ninety minutes of me – there will be no escape whatsoever! When the curtain goes up, the show is all about Elaine Stritch, and guess what? I've got the lead!

What are the skills you most admire in other actors? Are there any particular actors who have exerted an influence on how you perform?
Discipline, humility, understanding, generosity, unselfishness and

humour. If anyone knows of such an actor, get them to call me.

How much research do you undertake for a role?
I do not undertake any research; I learn my lines and listen to the director.

How do you prepare mentally and physically for a performance?
I suit up, show up (early), check my blood glucose, shoot up (insulin – scared you for a minute, didn't I?!), say a quick prayer and I'm there.

What were your most and least challenging roles?
There is no such thing as a 'least challenging role' because if a role is not a challenge, you should not have accepted it in the first place. My most challenging role is every single one I have ever played.

Which directors have you responded to most creatively?
Erwin Piscator, my first teacher; Harold Clurman; George Abbott; Noël Coward, certainly; Harold Prince; and, most recently, Gerald Gutieras. I extend my heartfelt thanks to him in particular for *A Delicate Balance*.

What do you think are the most productive rehearsal conditions?
More time, good coffee and skimmed milk.

Who are the most useful critics of your acting, and do you read critical reviews of your work?
I read every single review that has ever been written about me and I don't believe actors who say they do not. A bad review fills me with sadness, remorse and depression, but I am happy to say I rarely experience that sadness, remorse and depression. I think the most frightening review I have ever had just left me in a state of wonder. It was my first season of summer stock and I was playing the role of Amanda in Noël Coward's *Private Lives* (1950). I was in my early twenties, but apparently managed to convince the audience that I was at least thirty-five or forty. My review in the local paper was glowing; however, the last line scared me to death: 'Elaine Stritch has one problem: she just may have too much talent.' Those words really frightened me. I have come to realize talent is a glorious gift. Too much talent is downright dangerous, but to be honest, I kind of like the sound of it!

What are your views about the future of the profession?
I am sad that the straight play is losing its power. George S. Kaufman called the theatre 'the fabulous invalid'; well said, Mr Kaufman, and I firmly believe that the straight play will gain its power again. The musical comedy as I knew it seems to have had it, so I hope Mr Kaufman is right again about that. Regarding the musical comedy of today, well, I don't mind going to see *Les Miserables*, *Miss Saigon*, et cetera, et cetera, et cetera, but I want more *Guys and Dolls*, *Chicago* and Sondheim.

When the straight play does regain its position in the American theatre, I would be grateful for fewer four-letter words. Don't get me wrong, I've been known to kick a few around, but too much of anything loses its meaning, and if we go on much longer with this interview, it will do the same thing. Enough already! And thank you for listening.

Indira Varma

Indira Varma was born in 1973 and grew up in Bath. She trained at RADA. She has worked in theatre, film and television. Her theatre work includes *As You Like It* (1996), *Othello* (1997–8), directed by Sam Mendes, *The Three Sisters* (1999), *Celebration* (2000), directed by Harold Pinter, *The Country* (2000) and *Remembrance of Things Past* (Royal National Theatre, 2000–1). Her film credits include *Kama Sutra*, *Clancy's Kitchen*, *Sixth Happiness*, *Jinnah*, *Mad Dogs* and *Zehn Wahnsinnige Tage*. For television her credits include *The Whistle Blower*, *Attachments*, *Other People's Children*, *Land of Plenty* and *Psychos*.

What was your training?

I went to the Royal Academy of Dramatic Art (RADA) straight from school, at the age of seventeen. At school, I was pressed to go to university and for a time I felt that I might have missed out on acquiring the sorts of analytical skills a degree can provide, but I wanted to act and I made a decision based on what my instincts told me. In my year at RADA, only a handful of us came directly from school; most students were in their mid-twenties or older. It was difficult because it was my first time away from home, and because I didn't know London very well. I chose RADA for its solid classical foundation in acting, though I'm sure that every one of us privately believed that they were 'the mistake' that RADA had made.

I'm not steeped in British culture and I've often found that I don't share the popular references that may be used by a company of actors in a rehearsal room. Though I was brought up in Bath, my father's mother tongue is Hindi and my mother's first languages are French and German; they don't speak each other's languages and I spent a lot of time in either India or Switzerland, so when we went to watch any kind of entertainment we had to select something that we could all understand. As a result, I saw a great deal of Indian and classical dance, and I grew to love mime. Since childhood, I've had a fascination for the power of expression and communication, whether using language, the body, music or visual effects.

I was very stimulated by working with people of different ages at

RADA. We studied Method acting, of which I understood little at the time but found that a year or so after graduation the learning 'settled' and I had time to absorb what I'd been exposed to. I loved the physical and vocal classes, and my view today is that everyone should have the chance to do courses like the ones offered at RADA; we understand so little about ourselves and our anatomies and I left with a much greater knowledge of who I am.

Do you follow a particular technique?
No. My ideas are far from formed. There are so many different theories and methods of acting that can be explored. I'm in the early stages of my career and have so much more to learn. I certainly found Peter Brook's *The Empty Space* fascinating and I think David Mamet's books *A Whore's Profession* and *True and False* are thrilling because they turn the traditional idea of the drama school on its head and argue that acting is instinct. An acting course only provides a foundation, and I may have learned about the Method but you can only actually learn how to apply or adapt any technique when you begin to work professionally. I suspect it probably takes at least ten years of professional work for an actor to develop strong ideas about the ways they like to work. A few weeks ago, I met a friend who said that she had a solid method of acting based on Grotowski's ideas – for a moment I envied her certainty. I suppose I regard the Method as a safety net, but I have approached each of my characters and performances differently.

You acted in Harold Pinter's Celebration. *What was it like to work with Pinter?*
Before I went to audition, I read the play and didn't understand it. I always ask myself why characters say the things they do, but I just couldn't answer why with *Celebration*. For the audition, I sat at a table with the casting director and Harold Pinter, who expected me to plunge into the scene and read it straight away. This was all he required and I felt that I'd not shown my potential. Outside the audition room, I told the casting director of my disappointment and said I felt that I could simply have done anything, and that I had not been asked to show my range or to demonstrate that I could take instruction from a director. The casting director went back and relayed this to Pinter, and he replied that I had got the part. I don't know what he was looking for, but he knew when he'd found it!

On the first day of the second week, a point when most directors are just getting off the ground, Pinter asked the cast to do a run-through of the entire play; none of us had a clue what we were doing and it was very unnerving. Actors feel they need a more solid foundation in order to do a run-through and, because we still didn't understand the play, we felt that we couldn't speak the lines meaningfully. Pinter worked a lot through simple repetition of certain sections and was very particular about being faithful to the text. He gave small directions infrequently, such as 'speed up the lines' or 'leave a beat here', and I found that these small instructions often made larger issues or structures fall into place. He trusted his actors, which was very liberating – especially since he'd written the play – and he did not give exposition. Members of the cast would ask 'What does this line mean?' and he'd simply reply 'I don't know'. Many of us felt insecure about the process, but I felt as I went over the text again and again that I began to understand how to speak the words. I admired Pinter's democratic stance in rehearsals. Some of the actors had worked with him before, so there was a potential for an unevenness of status to develop, but every part was important to him, no matter how small. For example, there were two actors whose function was to fetch and remove plates and they were treated no differently from speaking cast members. Whilst my experiences of theatre have all been good, I know many actors who have felt marginalized in rehearsals.

Did you ever understand your part?
I probably imposed an understanding on it. My character was called Sonia and I found that the doing of it, and the energy and the speed required of the role, made me feel a certain way. I invented a narrative for myself about why she said things in a certain way in order to be able to remember how to deliver the line the next time; sometimes you'd find that the narrative would lose its value for you and you'd have to alter something slightly to keep fresh – it could either improve the moment or you'd feel you'd missed the mark. There was always a certain element of risk and chance because so much of the energy was in listening and responding to the other actors on-stage. The rehearsals for *Celebration* were set apart from one another, so during the week we met on a Monday, Wednesday and Friday from 2 to 6 p.m. It made the process seem fragmented, but in fact it allowed the actors to talk to each other between rehearsals and gave us all time to reflect, which was very valuable.

At the same time as you were appearing in Celebration, *you were rehearsing at the Royal Court in a play directed by Katie Mitchell. How did Mitchell's process compare?*

I can't think of two directors who work in such polar-opposite ways! The play was Martin Crimp's *The Country* and Crimp is generally understood to have been strongly influenced by Pinter's plays. Katie asked the actors to do a huge amount of research. I had to read Virgil because my character picks up a volume of his work in the play. We had to notate every fact we could extract from the play, or make a note of textual clues which might lead to revelation about plot or character. In every scene we had to be clear about what time of day it was and what our character might have been doing immediately before. We had to write the biographies of characters and decide when they had been born, which school they had attended, what their social life was like and what their relationship with their parents might be. The biographies had to tally with the other characters in terms of when we'd first met one another, so we wrote them together. Basically, we were asked to apply a form of psychoanalysis to our characters and of course we invented a great deal. In my case, I was trying to explore what might have led my character to want a relationship with an older man. We did this research for the first week and also did improvisation to explore certain aspects of the characters. Katie led visualization exercises: I had to visualize the flat in New York that my character referred to and pic-ture the character's set of friends in New York. Personally, I didn't find visualization exercises which were outside the world of the play particu-larly useful, but those set within the world of the play were helpful; for example, I had to visualize the trees that Rebecca sees and I found that this did stimulate my imagination. We did explore the meaning of lines with Katie, and on the elusive lines we simply made decisions about meaning. There was no concentration on the rhythm of the lines or the sound of the dialogue as there was with Pinter, though I found myself wishing that we could do work on rhythm. I suppose the main differ-ence between Pinter and Mitchell as directors is that all the research we did on *The Country* in the rehearsal room, we did outside the rehearsal room and for ourselves with *Celebration*.

I enjoyed the improvisation work with Katie Mitchell; frequently she'd ask a question about your character and if you couldn't find an answer we'd improvise and search for a solution. I remember one scene which is permeated with a strained atmosphere, when my character is in the living-room of her lover's house and meets her lover's wife. It isn't clear from the text if I know who she is, whether she knows about my character or if one of us is keeping something from the other. We improvised many different scenarios, and because my character was textually dominant in that scene, we made decisions which brought out my dominance.

What other acting exercises have you found useful?
For *Othello*, director Sam Mendes used an exercise that I'd learned at RADA called the whispering exercise: this involves two people who sit facing each other with two whisperers behind each of them. One whisperer speaks lines of dialogue into the ear of one of the seated actors and the actor has to communicate the lines, seeking to connect with the other seated actor. The other whisperer then speaks lines into the ear of the other actor, and likewise the actor has to give and respond to the person opposite. What you discover is that we all have a natural impulse to communicate. It's also an exercise about listening, and listening is a critical part of acting. Finding a reaction and response depend upon being able to hear and compute what the other actor is saying on all sorts of levels. Too many actors show off their elocution skills rather than speak with intent.

Mendes also asked us to act each other's parts during the first week of rehearsal, so we swapped roles with the actor with whom we had a main scene. I was playing Bianca, so I swapped parts with Cassio. I found it very interesting to inhabit the other character and it brought new and unexpected insights into the scene. Mendes also did a lot of language work with us: we would all learn Othello's speeches and deliver them by speaking a line each; it made everyone feel included and valued and it also helped us to understand Othello. The production toured round the world and it was an exciting time. My part was small and in a way that can be very nerve-racking. I had to wait an hour before I went on-stage and I couldn't afford to get anything wrong; playing a small part means that you can't show the development of a character or their different aspects. I played the part for a year and at one point Sam Mendes told me that he could see the enormous work I'd put into the role, that I'd made it an intricate oil painting, full of detail, but that I was pulling focus from the play and needed a much more straightforward approach. It was frustrating to reduce my performance but I absolutely respected his point. One of the most useful notes we were given, as a company, once we had 'passed' press night with flying colours and got great reviews, was 'Don't play the success'. That remark made quite an impression on me.

You're working on Pinter's adaptation of Proust's Remembrance of Things Past. *How is it?*
It's a cast of twenty-four and the plot of all six novels spans thirty years, so all the characters age. The abstraction of the novels has been translated into physicality and the director, Di Trevis, stresses the importance of ensemble work, so there's great emphasis on working and moving together as a group. We've done a lot of physical exercises that are connected to the era – for example, waltzing, which improves our co-ordination and makes us think about our own movements in relation to others on-stage. The director allotted 150 pages of Proust to each of us, and we have to become the masters of those pages; we have to note the colours, the smells, the food, the names of flowers and the characteristics of the characters. The aim is that when we're all in rehearsals together, we're a living Proust library and can all act as readers and researchers for each other. I think it's a brilliant idea and it really binds us together as a team.

What is your experience of film?
Acting for film and television follows the same principle as acting for the stage; you are still trying to find a truthfulness, but the scale is different and you have to imagine that the camera can *see* your thoughts, whereas in theatre you are generally communicating your thoughts directly. For film and television, you're often told to 'bring it down' and I suppose I love theatre acting because I find the challenges greater.

I've had lukewarm experiences with film and television and have been very disappointed by the poor quality of the scripts. In theatre, the play is the vehicle for the medium, and in film the visuals dominate; my experience is that the pictures may be beautiful but little else is impressive. In some ways I've been lucky to land parts, and my half-Asian identity has worked in my favour and secured me roles. On the other hand, I've also been typecast as the Asian babe, a bit of exotic, the corner-shop girl, or the London Asian girl. One of the more interesting roles was in a film called *Jinnah* (1998), where I played the wife of the father of Pakistan, Mohammed Ali Jinnah, but film is even more obsessed with looks than the theatre industry and casting directors generally don't consider me for roles which are non-Asian.

My first experience of film was the lead role in a film called *Kama Sutra* (1995–6) and I won the part while I was still at RADA. I spent four months filming in India with the director Mira Nair. I'd said beforehand that I thought the script needed a lot of attention and was assured that it would be improved, but I was so green about the outside world and I had no idea what to expect. In fact, the script was not changed, there was a lot of nudity in the film and a few sex scenes, and the experience really disillusioned me: it was beautifully shot but the narrative was weak. Film requires you to conform to a type and revolves around appearance; as a woman, you have to be slim and conform to a certain standard of beauty. I find this utterly frustrating. I've recently felt that in television I've been cast as a gesture towards the Asian community, and I am baffled about how I am meant to break in to roles.

Are you aware of actors who have influenced you?
Not specifically. I'm impressed and inspired by actors like Julie Walters and Frances McDormand. I saw Marcel Marceau as a child and thought he was astonishing; he could express something simple but profound just by moving his left shoulder. I find Theatre de Complicite's work very exciting and I enjoy a lot of physical theatre on the fringe. I find that much of the acting in the Royal Shakespeare Company is from the head up; in England, actors are not trained to be physical. At drama school we learn to think about the difference between what the characters say and what they mean, the difference between who a character is in private and who they are in public. We need to develop the same range of vocabularies for the physical. In film they cast superficially and according to appearance, but physically an actor can create many personae and give an entirely different view of themselves from any surface impression.

Can you say more about your frustrations with the preoccupation with appearance in film and theatre?
It's not just a matter of appearance. I've come across some unfortunate opinions in radio too. One producer cast me for a play and I asked what kind of Indian accent she wanted and which part of India was being represented through the voice. The reply was simply: 'Oh, general will do'!

At RADA, I think I rebelled for a while against the idea of the slim, beautiful thing; I dressed down and put on weight. But for the filming of *Kama Sutra* I had to lose weight in order to represent what was required of me; I'd got the lead part and it would have been foolish to turn it down. I've found that some casting directors, predominantly in television and film, seem to lack imagination, casting solely on the basis of a person's looks and therefore obstructing a good actor from the right job because they don't fit a cliché. On one occasion I was auditioned for a play and re-called but knew that I wasn't ready for such a large part and that I needed to build up my confidence more slowly. I rejected the part, but the casting director lambasted me and was not interested in my personal development as an actor. I think there are certain myths about actors' apprenticeships: many work very hard and are very talented but the industries still have structural prejudices and actors who are from non-white backgrounds can find it very tough. I am very lucky to be in my twenties and to have worked with the people I have in theatre; I have learned so much from individual directors and it is directors who have given me the chances to prove myself. I do value my experiences in theatre; but even from within, the theatre industry is quite shuttered. I often ask myself how one can meet Mike Leigh, Ken Loach or Steven Berkoff.

Do you read criticism?
I think spectators are increasingly frightened to have their own opinions; they want to be led. Actors depend on critics to encourage audiences and one small, offhand comment can be very destructive. Audiences now seem to believe everything they read. I don't read reviews. They are rarely either objective or universal. I was told during *The Country* that I had received great notices, but I thought: that was yesterday and it was one person's opinion, what matters is how I perform today.

What are your ambitions as an actor?
I hope that I can go on working with actors of longstanding experience because I learn a great deal from them. In *The Country*, my character had a higher status in the play than Juliet Stevenson's and it took me until the previews to work up the courage to meet her performance, but it was a great learning curve for me.

I'd love to have a good experience in film. There are brilliant directors, but because of the way the industry works, I don't feel I've had a chance to show my potential. I want to scream out what everyone knows: that beauty is not skin-deep. Why are women still suffering from the beauty myth? I wish film directors would have more courage. Gerard Depardieu and Daniel Auteuil are not classically good looking but they are immensely skilled actors, and that's what should count above everything.

Acknowledgements

The editors would especially like to thank John Barton, Anne Barton, Mike Cordner, Julie Crofts, David Edgar, John Lennard, Roger Luckhurst, Simon Mills, Caraid O'Brien, Julia Pascal, Lloyd Trott, Michael Slater and Ingrid Wassenaar.